I0409394

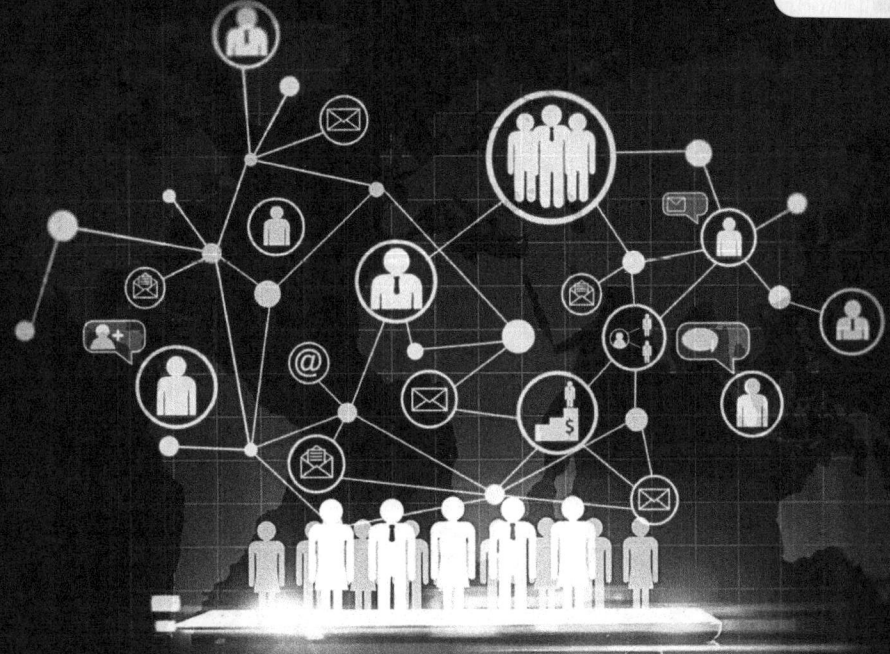

HUMAN RESOURCE MANAGEMENT

Policies & Process
You Will Be HR Expert After Reading

RUNWAY STUDIO

Human Resource Management Policies & Processes

Contents

HR General Organization Credo

We believe that our first and most important concern
is our customers; we believe that we should provide them with superior products and services with fair prices on time.

We also believe that our employees will grant or deprive us from being a market leader; we therefore must respect their dignity and recognize their merit. They deserve fair compensation, healthy and safe working conditions.
Our responsibility to our society is not of less importance, we aim to be an environment friendly industry and to maintain and protect our natural resources.To assume previous responsibilities, we must keep on working for a successful and profitable industry. Reducing costs and expenses - but not reducing quality, continues research, launching new products, all of which to guarantee fair return and success to our establishment.

ORGANIZATION MISSION

STATEMENT

Our mission is a (Technology).products group with a strong tradition of discovery. Our regional businesses are constantly evolving and continually searching for new and better ways to use our human, technological, and financial resources to improve the quality of life of people

Products or Services

Providing our customers with (Products or Services) which will meet their needs & expectations.

Concern of Employees

Enabling our employees "Becoming all they can be" by developing their careers, compensate them with competitive remunerations and fringe benefits, commensurate with their contributions toward efficient group operations.

Customers

Honorably serving the needs of the community by providing products and services of an excellent quality at a fair price on time to our customers based on our strong belief that "Our Customers Deserve the Best".

Concern for Survival

To be market leader in Egypt by serving the regional need for our products & services at a fair profit by producing, and distributing valuable products in a way that benefits our customers, employees, and our society.

HR Mission

Human Resources strive to be business partner in all Organization activities alongside with its staff members by creating sustainable competitive advantage through recruiting, developing, motivating & retaining highly skilled and loyal individuals, who will exert their maximum efforts and creativity to achieve organization 's strategies & dreams.

Transition of HR Development Strategy

To	From
Strategic	Operational
Qualitative	Quantitative
Partners	Policy
Long Term	Short Term
Consultant	Administrative
Business Orientation	Function Orientation
Proactive	Reactive
Solution oriented	Focused on Activities

Functions of HRM

Job Analysis / Desc.

Personnel Planning and Recruiting
Training and Development

Appraising Performance

Managing Careers

Establishing Pay Plans

Benefits and Services

Pay for Performance and Financial Incentives

Employee Safety and Health

HR Organizational Chart

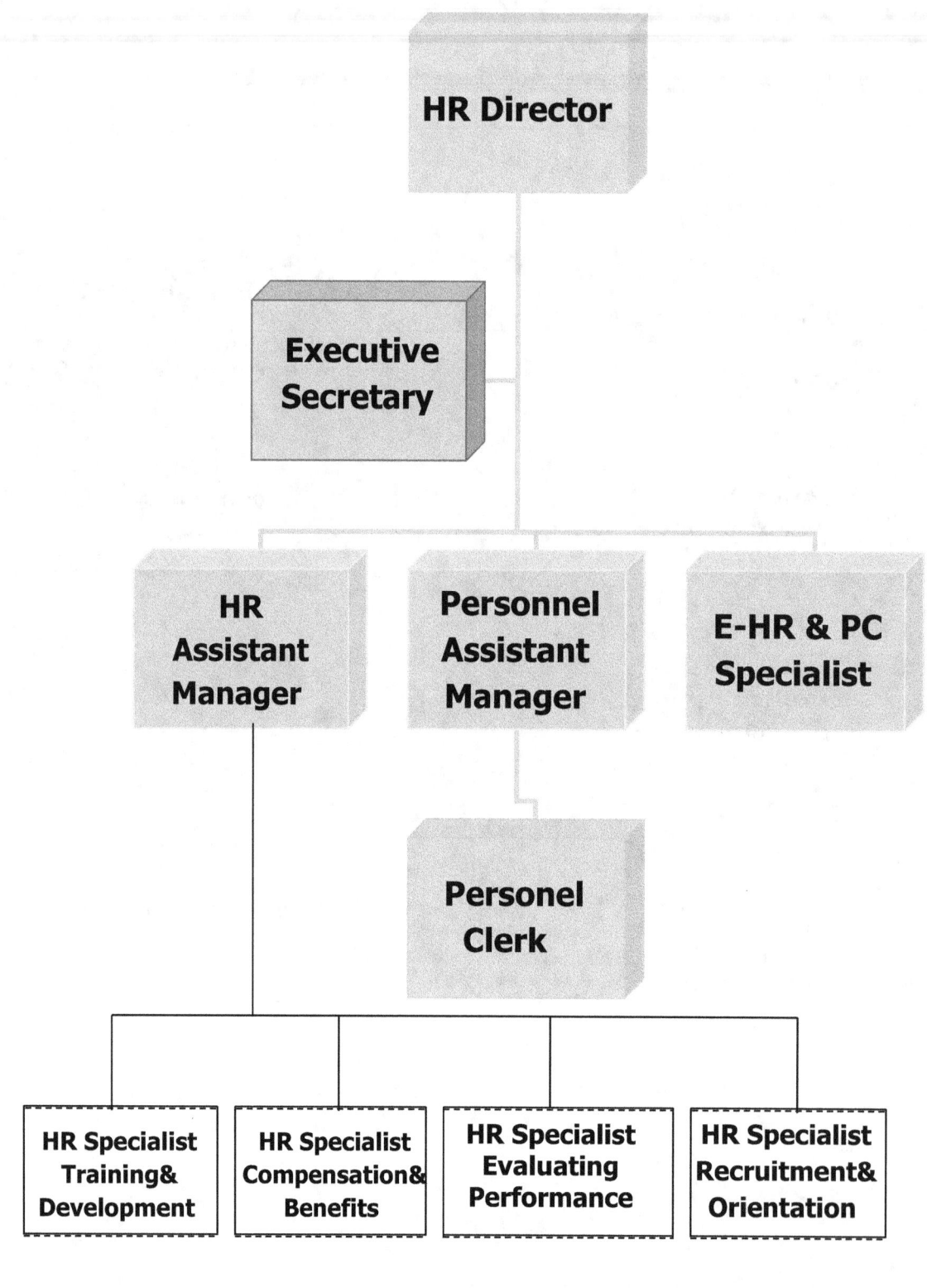

```
┌─────────────────────────────────────────────────┐
│                    ┌──────────────────────────┐  │
│                    │      HR Director          │  │
│                    └──────────────────────────┘  │
│   ┌──────────────────────────┐                   │
│   │      Executive           │                   │
│   │      Secretary           │                   │
│   └──────────────────────────┘                   │
└─────────────────────────────────────────────────┘
```

Responsibilities:

1. Responsible for all department's in/out correspondence.
2. Prepare monthly ideal employee lists.
3. Prepare department's monthly achievement report.
4. Prepare vacancies ads.
5. Receive applicants CV's.
6. Arrange applicant's interviews with HR director.
7. English/Arabic translation for department's documents & correspondence.
8. Prepare monthly news letter together with HR Director and
HR Senior Assistant.

HR Director

Personnel Assistant Manager

Responsibilities:

1. Responsible for all social insurance work in compliance with
social insurance law.
2. Preparing social insurance form for new employees (form no.1) & its attachments.
3. Preparing social insurance form for resigned employees (form no.6).
4. Preparing social insurance (form no.2) & its attachments.
5. Review employee's probation period reports.
6. Coordinates department's governmental relations.
7. Revise monthly wages to insure its compliance with Organization rules & regulations.
8. Responsible for issuing and delivering labor bureau cheques.
9. Reviewing annual raise sheets & applying it according to Organization policy
10. Revise periodical incentives reports.
11. Follow up and renew employees' contracts.
12. Arrange, follow up issuing and renewing official documents of the group.

HR Director

HR Assistant Manager

Responsibilities:

A) Coordinates & communicates HR activities with all locations

B) Assists Group HR Director in the following functions & activities:

o Processes, Policies & procedures related to HR functions.

o Computerizes forms, and facilitates all HR functions to produce an Electronic HR System.

o Analyses performance appraisal for training needs & development.

o Organizes training sessions both internally & externally.

o Organizes orientation programs for new employees.

o Prepares orientation booklet of group for new employees & Group HR Manual.

o Screens resumes for required job vacancies.

o Conducts interviews for applicants with HR Director.

o Assists Group –HR Director with all HR-related issues such as job description, recruiting, performance appraisal …..ETc.

o Initiates & organizes staff training activities (needs analysis, arrange in-house & outside training courses, develop post courses evaluation forms).

o Career development plans.

o Prepares HR- related presentations.

HR Director

E-HR & PC Specialist

Responsibilities:

1. Establish, renew & follow up employees' database.
2. Responsible for HR system (HRIS).
3. Responsible for issuing employees ID cards.
4. Executes an online HR manual on Organization's internal network.
5. Assists HR staff in any activity related to HR system such as: payroll, electronic timekeeping …)

HR Director

Personnel Assistant Manager

Personnel Clerk

Responsibilities:
1. Compile, copy, sort, and file records of office activities, business transactions, and other activities.
2. Operate office machines, such as photocopiers and scanners, facsimile machines , datashow.
3. Maintain and update filing, mailing, and database systems, either manually or using a computer.
4. Deliver messages and run errands.
5. Type, format, proofread and edit correspondence and other documents, from notes or dictating machines, using computers or typewriters.
6. Any other office administrative work.

HR Director

HR Specialist

Responsibilities:

1. Implements HR activities within the organization in coordination with HR Director.
2. Assists Group HR Director in the following functions & activities:
a. Personnel activities (payroll, timekeeping, vacations, employees' database...)
b. Processes, Policies & procedures related to HR functions.
c. Computerizes forms, and facilitates all HR functions to produce an Electronic HR System.
d. Analyses performance appraisal for training needs & development.
e. Organizes training sessions both internally & externally.
f. Organizes orientation programs for new employees.
g. Screens resumes for required job vacancies.
h. Conducts interviews for applicants.
i. Assists Group -HR Director with all HR-related issues such as job
description, recruiting, performance appraisal …..Etc.
j. Initiates & organizes staff training activities (needs analysis, arrange in-house & outside training courses, develop post courses evaluation forms).
k. Career development plans.
l. Prepares HR- related presentations.

PART ONE
ORGANIZATION'S STANDARDS &
ETHICS

1- Code of Ethics:

The organization's code of conduct applies to every employee and provides employees with guidance in maintaining the ethical and cultural values and standards of the organization that help protect its reputation:

o Honesty:
Organization's Employees May Not:
- Have potential to, pay or receive any bribes in order to obtain or maintain business.
- Carry out any act of dishonesty or intentionally misrepresent the facts in any business transaction.
- Falsify corporate records, hide improper activities or fail to accurately reflect the organization's business.

o Political and Community Activities and Contributions:
The organization is not active in politics and does not make political contributions; employees may participate on an individual basis only, and outside the organization premises.
The organization encourages employees and managers to practice their responsibility as private citizens and not as organization employees.

o Conflict of Interest:
The organization's conflict of interest policy is clear: Do not compete with its business, and never let your work at the organization be influenced by personal or family interests.

o Accounts and Record Keeping:
Our business files must reflect all components of transactions. Appropriate records must be kept of all transactions. It is the responsibility of the employee to maintain these standards. Employees are expected to co- operate fully with our internal and external accountants/ auditors. Information must not be falsified or concealed under any circumstances and an employee whose activities will cause false financial reporting will be subject to disciplinary action.

o Disclosure:

Every employee shall disclose directly to his/ her manager any personal situation or transaction that may be in conflict with the organization's code.

2- Place of Work:

Your place of work will be as stated in your letter of employment. However, on occasions, the organization may require you to visit or work in another location related to the organization or work.

3- Dress code:

It is important that the organization presents a courteous, smart and efficient image. Personal appearance and dressing of employees is one vital element. Employees are expected to adhere to organization uniform during working hours. Employees who have not predefined uniform are expected to be appropriately and neatly dressed in business clothes in addition to a neat tie at all times, and should not wear jeans or casual clothes. Employees are required to maintain a high standard of cleanliness and personal hygiene. Employees are also not expected to be chewing a gum inside the office.

4-Personal data:

Any change to your personal details during your employment should be notified to the Human Resources Department. Any personal data on employees is always treated as confidential.

5-Gifts to or from third parties:

The giving or accepting of favors/gifts to or from a client, potential client, supplier or potential supplier of goods or services to the organization is not permitted unless what is given is of nominal value, or if refusal to accept would be considered discourteous or harmful to the organization. "Nominal" in this context means less than L.E. 50. If the value of the gift, favor or benefit exceeds L.E. 50, approval must be taken from your manager. Employees may accept and keep items of, for example calendars, block notes, stationary…etc

6-Health and Safety:

The organization is committed to providing a safe and healthy work environment and to comply with all applicable environmental, safety, and health laws and regulations.

The organization is dedicated to developing, maintaining, and operating facilities that protect our people and physical resources and to ensuring that work is done safely according to established safety codes and procedures. It is the employee's responsibility to maintain and follow these safety standards.

7-Employee Involvement/ Organization Announcements:

Regular contact and exchanges of information between managers and employees are encouraged and will be maintained by team meetings. Organization announcements will be publicized through notice boards. Employees can also publish notices on these boards, in such case prior approval of HR Director is required.

8-Behavior and work performance:

Employees must maintain a polite, friendly, and cooperative attitude to one another and to avoid any conduct annoying or provoking to one another. At the work, each employee is required to work considerately and not to carry out any other activity. The following are prohibited at work:

o Sleeping or resting.

o Any criminal activity.

o Any behavior likely to outrage normal standards of morality and decency.

o Swearing or use of unpleasant or rude language.

o Language or behavior inappropriate to any segment of the population at large, whether sex, race, religion, nationality… etc

o Hitting another employee, with or without any object.

o Interfering in any way with any belongings of any employee or with any organization property entrusted to him.

Employees with any complaints concerning the behavior or treatment of another employee may make report to their manager or Human Resources department, which shall be treated in confidentiality.

9- Smoking:

Smoking is a considerable irritant to many people, in addition to being a serious health risk to both smoker and to those nearby. Smoking is therefore not allowed in all parts of the organization, smoking is allowed only outside the organization premises.

10- Communication:

Effective communication is the lifeblood of any efficient organization. One of the organization's aims is, therefore, to establish efficient and effective lines of formal and informal communication whilst at the same time reducing bureaucracy to a minimum.

Communication structure in the Organization is as follows:

o Manuals and documentation

o Reports

o Family Meetings

o Email

o Internet

o Notice boards

o Intranet

Part Two
Work Regulations

1- Working hours:

The organization expects the employees to be at work regularly and on time. The standard flexible working hours are from:

6 days/week locations:

Starting hour 8:30am – 9:00am

Leaving hour 5:00pm – 5:15pm

To avoid being penalized, every employee should satisfy full working hours per day with an hour break for praying, eating …etc within the office. In case of coming to work after 8.30 am or working hours is less than 9 hours per day, such day will be deducted from the annual leave of the employee. In case of lack of vacation balance; the day will be deducted from the monthly salary.

Although it is appreciated that many managerial staff works longer hours, they have to sign at the attendance sheet upon arrival and departure.

During Ramadan, working hours change. Changes in the working hours will be announced to all employees in advance.

The organization reserves the right to request different or additional hours of work if business requirements make this necessary.

2- Payment of Salary:

Salaries are stated in your letter of employment/contract and are paid monthly by the end of every month.

3- Personal Properties:

In case employees want to bring any material, documents, floppy disks, CDs or other stuff inside the organization, s/he has to register such stuff at the security office upon arrival to work in the morning.

4- Expenses:

All reasonable expenses incurred during business or travel outside organization may be paid back if receipts support them and are approved by the relevant authorized signature. Employees must not authorize their own expense claim. All employees are required to comply with the organization's expenses policy issued and adjusted from time to time by the Finance Dept. / HR Dept.

5- Organization's Transportation Policy:

Services' staff is allowed to use the company's bus for free while coming to & leaving from work.

6- Telephone System:

The organization expects employees to behave responsibly toward telephone calls, and recognizes that in certain circumstances personal calls need to be made. These should, however, be limited to emergencies or work matters, which necessitate the re-arrangement of personal matters. Also we have to bear in mind & realize that our customers need to call us.

PART THREE
POLICIES & PROCESSES

Personnel planning and Recruitment

1-Developing personnel plans requires three forecasts: one for personnel requirements, one for the supply of outside candidates, and one for the supply of inside candidates. To predict the need for personnel, first project the demand for the product or service. Next project the volume of production required to meet these estimates; finally, relate personnel needs to these production estimates.

2-.Once personnel needs are projected, the next step is to build up a pool of qualified applicants. We discussed

several sources of candidates, including internal sources (or promotion from within), advertising, employment

agencies, executive recruiters, college recruiting, the internet, and referrals and walk-ins. Remember that it is

unlawful to discriminate against any individual with respect to employment because of race, color, religion, sex,

national origin, or age (unless religion, sex, or

Origin is bona fide occupational qualifications).

3-The initial selection screening in most organizations begins with an application form. Most managers use these just to obtain background data. However, you can use application form data to make predictions about the applicant's future performance. For example, application forms have been used to predict job tenure, job success, and employee theft.

4-Personnel planning and recruiting directly affect employee commitment because commitment depends on hiring employees who have the potential to develop. And the more qualified applicants you have, the higher your selection standards can be. Selection usually begins with effective testing and interviewing, to which we now turn.

Employee Testing & Selection

1. In this chapter we discussed several techniques for screening and selecting job candidates

The first was testing.

2-test Validity answers the question, "What does this test measure we discussed criterion validity and content

validity. Criterion validity means demonstrating that those who do well on the test do well on the job; content

validity is demonstrated by showing that the test constitutes a fair sample of the content of the job.

3. as used by psychologists, the term reliability always means consistency. One way to measure reliability is to

administer the same (or equivalent) tests to the same people at two different points in time. Or you could focus on

internal consistency, comparing the responses to roughly equivalent items on the same test.

4-There are many types of personnel tests in use, including intelligence tests, tests of

Physical skills, tests of achievement, aptitude tests, interest inventories, and personality tests.

5- For a selection test to be useful scores should be predictably related to performance on the job; you must

validate the test. This requires five steps: (a) analyze the job, (b) choose your tests,

(c) Administer the test, (d)relate test scores and criteria (e)cross-validate and revalidate the test.

6- Under equal rights legislation, an employer may have to be able to prove that his or her tests are predictive of success or failure on the job. This usually requires a predictive validation study, although other means of validation are often acceptable.

7. Some basic testing guidelines include (a) use tests as supplement to, (b) validate.

The tests for appropriate jobs, (c) analyze all current hiring and promotion standards, (d) beware of certain tests, (e) use a certified psychologist, and (f) maintain good test conditions.

8. The work sampling selection technique is based on "the assumption that the best

Indicator of future performance is past performance." Here you use the applicant's

Actual performance on the same (or very similar) job to predict his or her future job performance. The steps are

(a) analyze applicant 's previous work experience (b)have experts list component tasks for job openings, (c) select

crucial tasks as work sample measures, (d) break down these tasks into steps, (e) test the applicant, and (f) relate

the applicant's work sample score to his or her performance on the Job.

9. Management assessment centers are a third screening device and expose applicants to a series of real-life exercise. Performance is observed and assessed by experts, who then check their assessments by observing the participants when they are back at their jobs. Examples of "real-life" exercises include a simulated business game, an in-basket exercise, and group discussions.

10. Even though most people prefer not to give bad references, most companies still carry out some sort of

reference check on their candidates. These can be useful in raising red flags, and structured questionnaires can

improve the usefulness of the responses you receive.

11. Other selection tools we discussed include the polygraph, honesty tests, graphology, and the physical examination.

Interviewing Candidates

There are several basic types of interviews: situational, nondirective, structured, sequential, panel, stress, and appraisal interviews. All interviews can be classified according to content, structure, purpose, and method of administration.

2. Several factors and problems can undermine the usefulness of an interview. These are making premature
decisions, letting unfavorable information predominate, and not knowing the requirements of the job, being under
pressure to hire, not allowing for the candidate-order effect, and sending visual cues to telegraph enthusiasm.

3. the five steps in the interview include: plan, establish rapport, question the candidate, close the interview, and review the data.

4. Guidelines for interviewers include: Use a structured guide, know the requirements of the job, focus on traits
you can more accurately evaluate (like motivation), let the interviewee do most of the talking, delay your decision
until after the interview, and remember the EEOC requirements.

5- The steps in a structured or situational interview are: job analysis, evaluate the job duty information, develop interview questions with critical incidents, develop benchmark answers, appoint an interview committee, and implement.

6. As an interviewee, keep in mind that interviewers tend to make premature decisions and let unfavorable
information predominate; your appearance and enthusiasm are important; you should get the interviewer to talk; it
is important to prepare before walking in-get to know the job and the problems the interviewer wants solved; and
you should stress your enthusiasm and motivation to work, and how your accomplishments match your interviewer's
needs.

7. a quick procedure for conducting an interview is to develop behavioral specifications; determine the basic intellectual, motivation, personality, and experience factors to probe for; use an interview plan; and then match the individual to the job... The procedure is especially useful in small firms with HR groups, but can be used in large firms as well.

8. Value-based hiring can contribute to building employee commitment. It assume5 that management has clarified
the values it cherishes (such as quality at Toyota) spends adequate time in the selection process, and provides for
realistic previews.

RECRUITMENT PROCESS

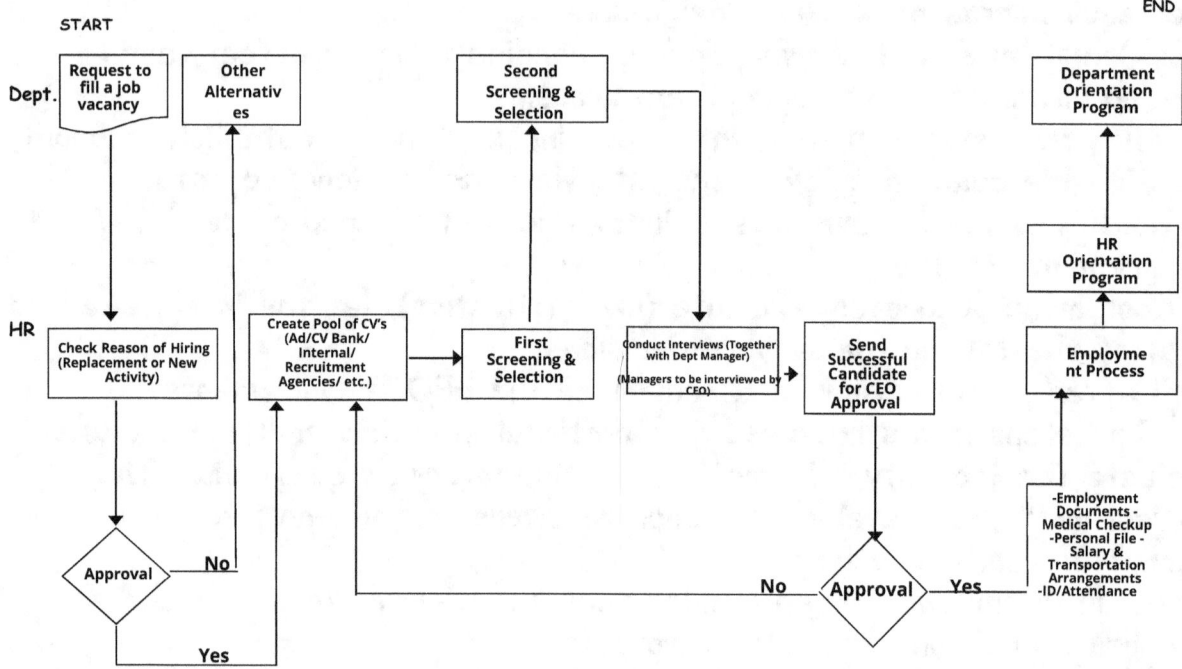

START

END

Dept.

Request to fill a job vacancy

Other Alternatives

Second Screening & Selection

Department Orientation Program

HR

Check Reason of Hiring (Replacement or New Activity)

Create Pool of CV's (Ad/CV Bank/ Internal/ Recruitment Agencies/ etc.)

First Screening & Selection

Conduct Interviews (Together with Dept Manager) (Managers to be interviewed by CEO)

Send Successful Candidate for CEO Approval

HR Orientation Program

Employment Process

Approval — No

Yes

No — Approval — Yes

-Employment Documents - Medical Checkup -Personal File - Salary & Transportation Arrangements -ID/Attendance

POLICY OF HIRING & RECRUITMENT

1-1 Prospective employees must submit all of the following documents to the Human Resources department within one week before joining the organization:

o Birth certificate or an official copy
o A copy of the identity card, family card or passport
o Certificate stating completion of military service or final exemption from it
o 4 passport – size photos
o Criminal record
o Academic certificate
o Form six of social insurance (for those who were previously employed)
o Registration certificate from manpower office

1-2 Failure to provide any of the above documents in full and accurate information as requested by Human Resources Dept. during the application process shall stop the employment process.

1-3 upon the completion of employee's hiring papers, the HR department sets the start date of the employee, and informs the head of the department and announces the hiring of the new employee through new employee announcement.

ORIENTATION AND TRAINING

1. In this chapter we focused on technical skills training for new employees and for present employees whose performance is deficient. For either, uncovering training requirements begins with analyzing the cause of the problem and determining the training that may be needed. Remember to ask whether it is a training problem or a more deep-rooted problem like poor selection or low wages.

2. The training process consists of five steps: needs analysis; instructional design; Validation; implementation; evaluation.

3. Some principles of learning theory include: Make the material meaningful (by providing a bird's-eye view and familiar examples, organizing the material, splitting it into meaningful chunks, and using familiar terms and visual aids); make provision for transfer of training; and try to motivate your trainee.

4. Job instruction training is useful for training on jobs that consist of a logical sequence of steps. Vestibule training combines the advantages of on- and off-the-job training.

5. On-the-job training is a third basic training technique. It might take the form of the understudy method, job rotation, or special assignments and committees. In any case, it should have four steps: preparing the learner, presenting the operation (Or nature of the job), doing performance tryouts, and following up. Other training methods include audiovisual techniques, lectures, and computer- assisted instruction.

6. in gauging the effectiveness of a training program there are four categories of out- comes you can measure: reaction, learning, behavior, and results. In some cases where training seems to have failed, it may be because training was not the appropriate solution.

ORIENTATION POLICY

2-1 on the first day of employment, the employee will sign starting work form.

The first part of the orientation is handled by HR department. The HR department will give the new employee the employee handbook and explain a brief about the organization, its departments and the flow of work

2-2 The second part of the orientation is handled by the department's manager who will introduce the employee to his/ her colleagues in the organization, familiarize the new employee with the workplace and explaining details about the organization and the job description.

POLICY OF PROBATION PERIOD

1. The HR department together with department head monitors employee attendance records during the three months of probation period, in addition to the overall observation of employee attitude and performance. Before completion of three months,

2. The department head should do a performance appraisal for employee.

3. The department head should then forward employee appraisal to the HR department.

4. The HR department will review the employee appraisal and will then put its recommendations in coordination with department head with regard to the following:

o Compensation review/ adjustments

o Insurance status

o Training needs

o Any uncommon situation, behavior, or performance during three-month probation period.

5. Employee appraisal and HR recommendations is forwarded to MD for review and action if required.

6. The HR will inform employee for any adjustments before the end of the probation period.

7. Those who have successfully completed the probation period will sign the contract.

8. Insurance also starts after the three-month probation period and is only granted for those who have successfully completed the probation period.

9. If employee failed to pass probation period successfully, s/he will be terminated immediately.

ORIENTATION PROGRAM &
PROBATION PERIOD EVALUATION

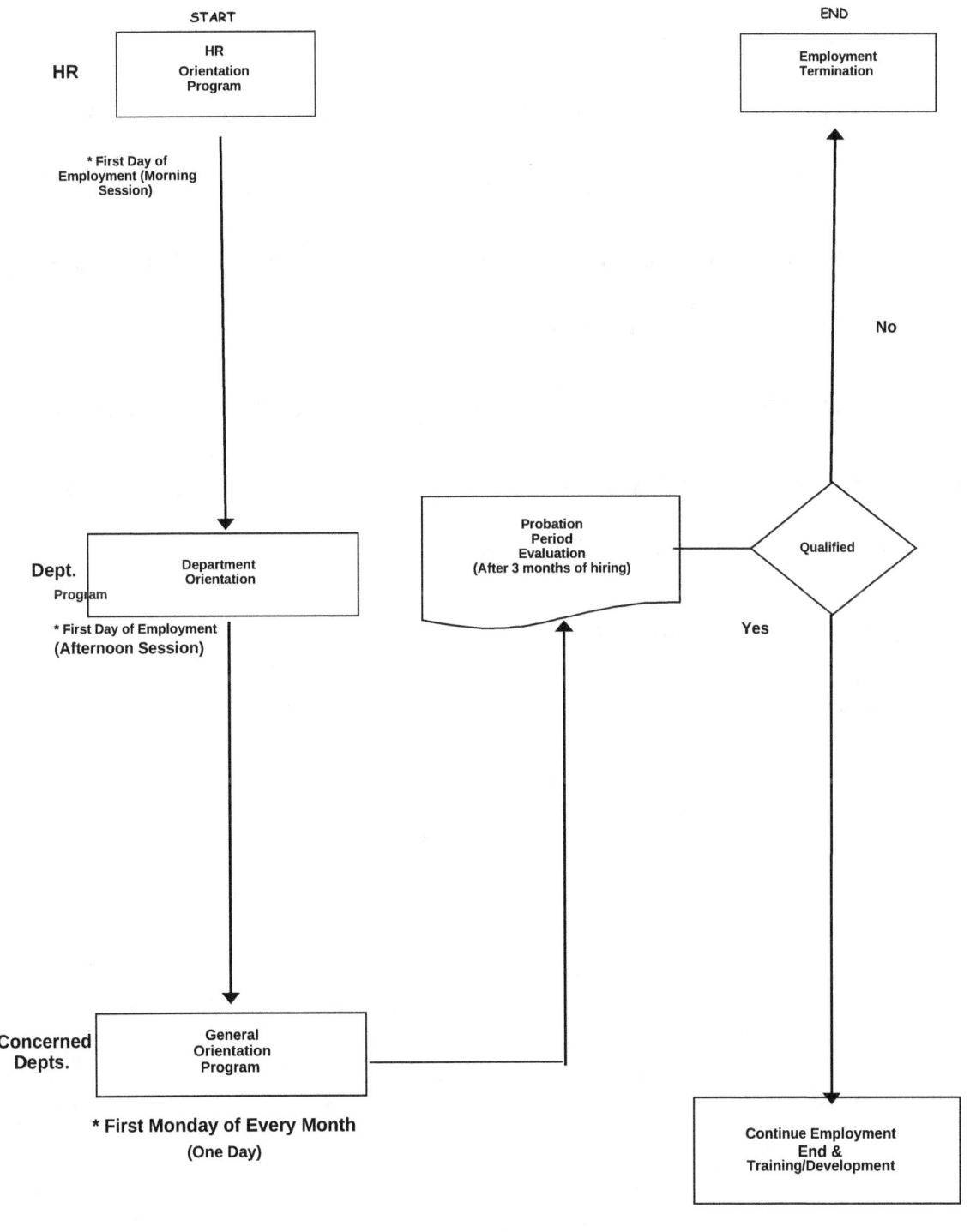

START

HR

HR
Orientation
Program

* First Day of
Employment (Morning
Session)

Dept.

Department
Orientation

Program

* First Day of Employment
(Afternoon Session)

**Concerned
Depts.**

General
Orientation
Program

* First Monday of Every Month
(One Day)

Probation
Period
Evaluation
(After 3 months of hiring)

Qualified

END

Employment
Termination

No

Yes

Continue Employment
End &
Training/Development

POLICY OF ATTENDANCE

All department heads must submit the monthly leaves plan to HR Dept.

a week before the beginning of each month.

All employees have to register their attendance (in/out) in the

attendance system used (cards, books, attendance machines…etc).

Late attendance will be calculated after 9:00 a.m. for staff.

The attendance penalty rules are monthly and are reset at the beginning

of each month.

Attendance penalties are handled according to Organization regulations

and labor law disciplinary procedures as mentioned in Disciplinary

Procedures section.

The HR dept. will provide every department head with a monthly

attendance report for all department staff at the end of every

month.

POLICY OF BUSINESS TRIPS

a- Internal business trips:

Procedures:

• Internal business trip form has to be signed by the department's manager and submitted to HR department one
day prior to its date.

• By the dept's manager approval, the business trips are
allowed in the same/ next day.

• In case of transportation expenses incurred during business trip, transportation expenses request has to be
signed by the dept's manager and submitted to Finance
Dept. to receive such expenses every two weeks.

b- International business trips:

• International business trip form should be signed by the Department Manager and Managing Director and submitted
to HR department two weeks prior to its date.

• Staff assigned to an international business trip is provided with an air ticket, transportation expenses from/to
airport, and suitable accommodation in the host country
(hotel B&B reservation).

• Staff are provided with a daily allowance (pocket money) equivalent to $/day. Daily allowance is reviewed regularly and is subject to change according to trip
destination.

• Daily allowance covers staff expenses inside host country
including: lunch, dinner, drinks.

• In case Host Organization does not provide transportation, staff transportation expenses are paid by the Organization.

• Phone calls should be very restricted and limited to business related affairs. Using private mobile phones is strongly recommended. Organization supply staff mobile phones with
roaming & international calls facilities.

POLICY OF VACATIONS

6-1 Annual Leave

• The period of annual leave is 21 days with full pay for those spent one complete year in the service, and increased to thirty days once the worker spends ten years in service with one or more employers, or for those over the age of 50 years old. The holidays, the official occasion's days off, the weekly days off is
not counted as part of the leave days.

• If the worker's service is less than one year, s/he is entitled to a leave in proportion to the period s/he has spent in work, providing he has spent six months in the service of the
employer.

• The employer determines the dates of the annual leave according to work exigencies and conditions. Employer should not interrupt the leave except for strong reason(s) necessitated by work
interests.

• The worker starts his leave on the date and for the period determined by the employer. If the worker refuses in writing to
go on leave, s/he forfeits his right to collecting their equivalent. In all cases the worker obtains an annual leave of
fifteen days including at least six continuous days.

• The worker has the right to determine the date of his /her annual leave if he is sitting for the exam in any educational stages, providing s/he notifies the employer at least fifteen
days before s/he goes on leave.

• The employer has the right to deprive the worker from his/her wage for the leave period, or retrieve the wage s/he has paid for it, if it is established that the worker has worked during leaves with another employer, without prejudice to the
disciplinary sanction.

6-2 Casual leave

The worker may abstain from work for casual reason for a period not exceeding six days during the year, with a maximum limit of two days each time. The casual leave is counted as part
of the annual leave determined for the worker.

6-3 Public & official holidays

The worker has the right to a paid leave on the following holidays:

Christmas (January 7th)

Arraft day, the first and second day of Greater Bairam (Eid Al-Adha)*

New Hijri year*

Feast of Prophet Muhammad's birth*

Liberation of Sinai (April 25th)

Labours' day (May the 1st)

Easter (sham el-Nasseim)

Revolution of July anniversary (July 23rd)

6th of October victory anniversary

The first & second day of Bairam (Eid El- Iftar)*

*Public holidays which are determined on their dates according to official announcement.

Public holidays for Christians only:

Resurrection day.

Palm Sunday

6-4 Pilgrimage/ visiting Mekka leave:

The worker spending five continuous years in the service of the employer has the right to a leave of one month with full pay for performing the religious pilgrimage duty, or visiting Mekka. That leave is granted only once through his/her service period.

6-5-Sick leave:

a- Commercial establishments:

The worker whose sickness is established has the right to a sick leave to be determined by the medical care provider assigned by the organization or the state medical insurance. During that period, s/he is entitled to a compensation wage as determined by the social Insurance Law as follows:-

· 75%of his/her salary during the first three months.

• 85% of his salary during the consecutive three months

b- Industrial installations:
The worker whose sickness is established has the right to which
are applicable the provisions of articles (1) and (8) of law No.21 for the
year 1958 on reorganization and encouragement
of industry, has the right to a sick leave every three years in
the services, on the basis of one month with full pay, then eight months
with a wage equivalent to (75%) of his salary, then three months without
pay, incase the medical care provider assigned by the organization or the
state medical insurance
decides the likelihood of his recovery.
The worker may benefit from his frozen annual leaves; besides
the sick leave to which he is entitled. He may also request transferring
the sick leave into an annual leave if he has a
balance allowing for doing so.

6-6 Maternity leave:
A female worker having spent ten months in the service of the
employer or more has the right to a paid maternity leave of ninety
days. Comprising the period before delivery and after parturition, she
submits medical certificate states the expected date of delivery, in
addition to the birth certificate of the
child.
The maternity leave is not entitled more than twice throughout
the female worker's period of service.

6-7 Child care leaves:
A female worker has the right to obtain an unpaid leave for a period
not exceeding two years, to care for her child. This leave is not
entitled more than twice throughout her service
period.

Procedures:
1-Annual Leave:
• The employee must submit a leave request
form to department head 5 days before its due date, all
department heads must take into consideration the balance of
leaves sheet sent by HR Dept. monthly to all departments.

All leave requests must be approved &
submitted to HR Dept. two days before their due date to
check vacation balance.

2-Casual leave:
All leave requests must be submitted to
department head on the same day of resuming work.
Upon approval of leave requests, all forms
must be sent to HR Dept. at the same day or on the next day
maximum.

Important remark:
In case of violating the above-mentioned procedures, the leave
period is considered as "leave without permission".

ESTABLISHING PAY PLAN-

1. There are two bases on which to pay employees compensation:
increments of time 'and volume production. The former includes hourly
or daily wages and salaries. Basing pay on volume of production ties
compensation directly to the amount of production .

2. Establishing pay rates involves five steps: conduct salary survey,
evaluate jobs, develop pay grades, use wage curves, and fine tune pay
rates;

3. Job evaluation is aimed at determining the
relative worth of a job. It compares jobs to one
another based on their content, which is usually
defined in terms of compassable factors like skills,
effort, responsibility, and working conditions.

4- The ranking method of job evaluation has five steps: (a) obtain job information, (b) select clusters of jobs to be rated, (c) select compassable factors, (d) rank jobs and, (e) (e) combine ratings (of several raters). This is a simple method to use; there is a tendency to rely too heavily on guesstimates. The classification (or grading) method is a second qualitative approach that categorizes jobs based on a c description or classification rules for each class.

5- The point method of job evaluation requires identifying a number of compensable factors and then determining the degree to which each of these factors is present in the job.

6. the factor comparison method, as explained in the appendix, is a quantitative job evaluation technique that entails deciding which jobs have more of certain condensable factors than others.

7. Most managers group similar jobs into wage or pay grades for pay purposes. These are comprised of jobs of approximately equal difficulty or importance as deter- mined by job evaluation.

8. The wage curve (or line) shows the average target wage for each pay grade (or job). It can help show you what the average wage for each grade should be, and whether any present wages or salaries are out of line. Developing a wage curve involves four steps: (a) find the average pay for each pay grade, (b) plot these wage rates for each pay grade, (c) draw the wage line, and (d) price jobs after plotting present wage rates.

9. Developing a compensation plan for executive,

managerial, and professional personnel is complicated

by the fact that factors like performance and

creativity must take precedence over static factors

like working conditions. Market rates, performance,

and incentives and benefits thus playa much greater

role than doe's job evaluation for these employees. 10. Broad banding

means collapsing salary grades

and ranges into just a few wide levels or bands,

each of which then contains a relatively wide range

of jobs and salary levels.

11. Four main compensation issues discussed were comparable worth, pay

secrecy, inflation, and cost- of-living differentials.

POLICY OF PAYROLL & OVERTIME

a- Payroll procedures:

Salaries are paid on the 29th of each month.
Current month salary updates (appraisal
results/deduction/raises) are due next month.
Performance appraisal forms & salary updates should
be submitted to HR on the 15th of each month to be
revised and sent to finance department.
Any salary adjustments should be reviewed and
approved from HR Director and MD.

b- Overtime policy:

It should be understood and known to all staff that the Organization
does not encourage overtime, but
only applied whenever work necessitate.
All employees are strongly recommended to perform their job duties
during normal working hours. This in
turn entails the following:
o The economic and wise use of daily working hours and the constant
controlling and supervision from the side
of department heads.
o Continues development for employees' performance in
order to increase their efficiency.
Eligibility:
Non-managerial staff, i.e. below grade "Manager".
In case managerial staff works full day during weekends or official
holidays, then they are entitled for full day vacation as a compensation
to be added
to their vacation balance.
Overtime policy is not applicable to sales staff.
Procedures:
· Each manager should submit overtime request form to HR department
indicating reason and economic justification for overtime, required number
of staff and expected period. This form should be submitted by the 20th
of each month to be
implemented in the next month.

HR Department reviews each department request to verify work needs and then sends approval/denial to
department head.
By the 15th of each month, time sheet forms signed
by department manager should be submitted to HR department to calculate overtime hours for payment
with monthly salary.
In all cases daily working hours should not exceed 10
hours/day.

Overtime calculation:
Morning overtime hours (from 07:00 am to 07:00
pm)= normal pay + 35%/hour
Night overtime hours (from 07:00 pm to 07:00 am)=
normal pay + 70%/hour

Official holidays= normal pay + 200%/day
Week end= normal pay + 100%/day + day off in the
next week

Payroll Process

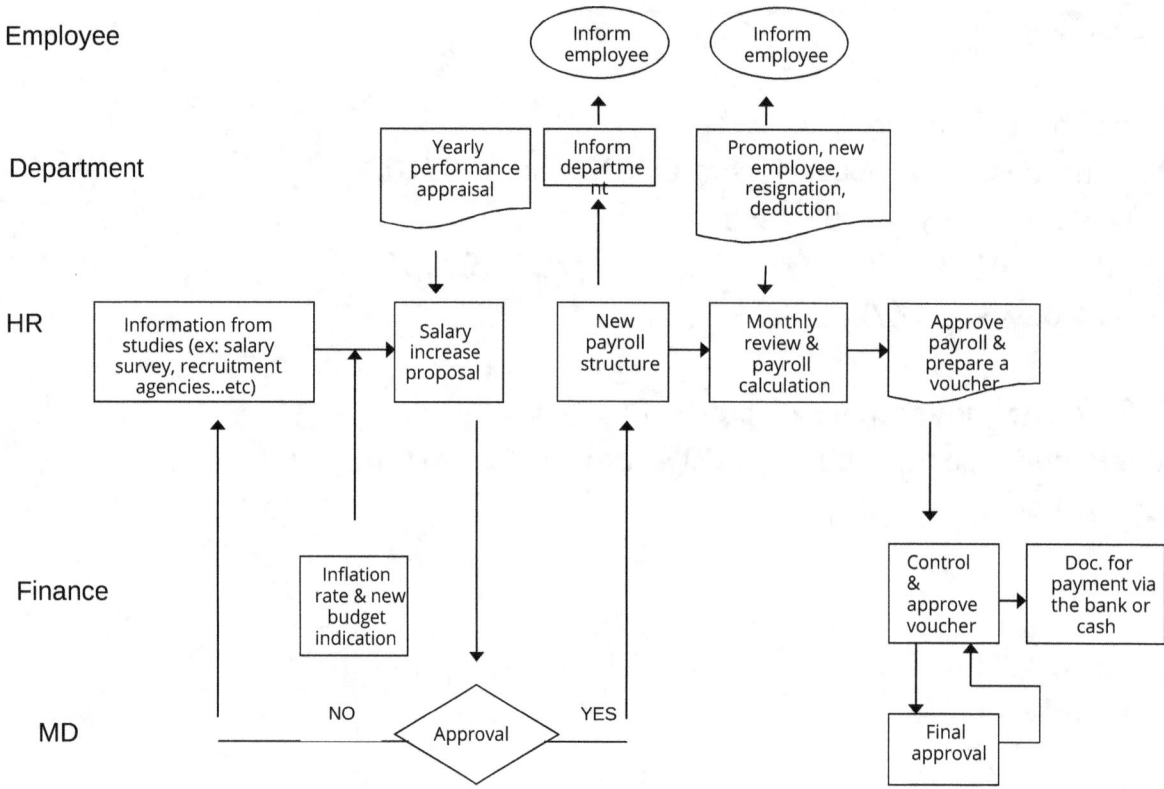

Employee

Department

HR

Finance

MD

Employee: Inform employee / Inform employee

Department: Yearly performance appraisal | Inform department | Promotion, new employee, resignation, deduction

HR: Information from studies (ex: salary survey, recruitment agencies...etc) | Salary increase proposal | New payroll structure | Monthly review & payroll calculation | Approve payroll & prepare a voucher

Finance: Inflation rate & new budget indication | Control & approve voucher | Doc. for payment via the bank or cash | Final approval

MD: Approval (NO / YES)

Overtime Process

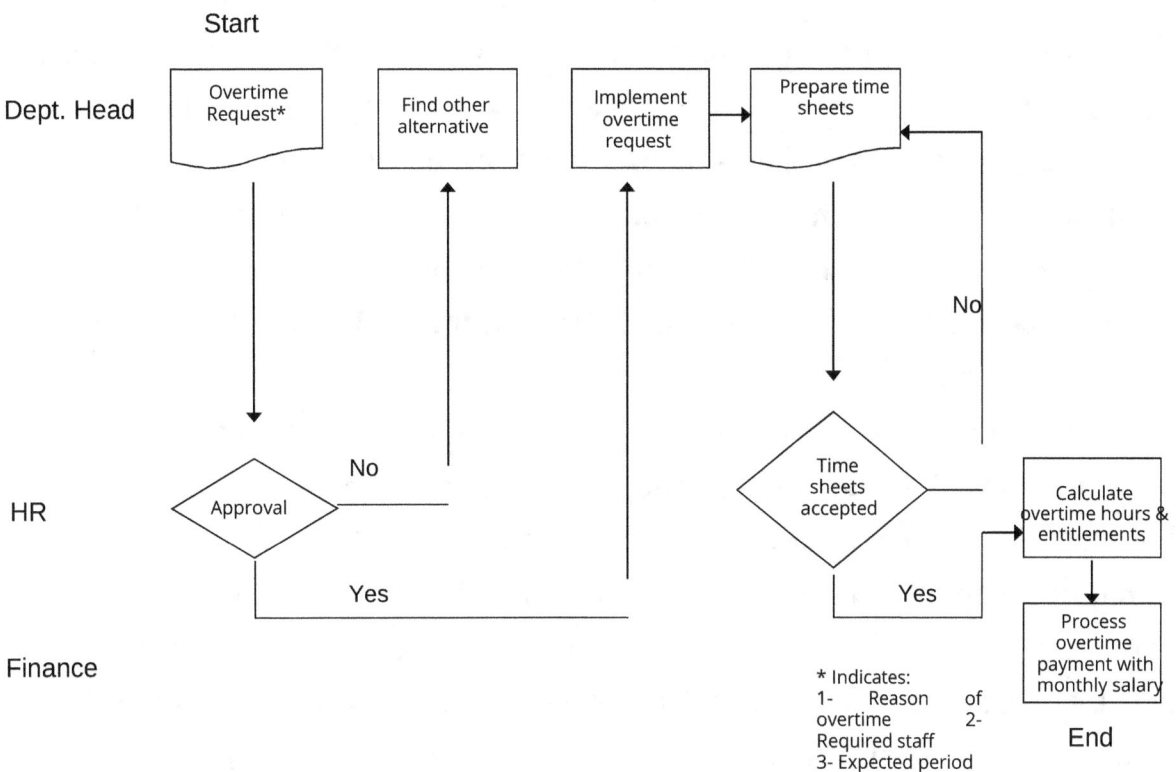

Start

Dept. Head

Overtime Request*

Find other alternative

Implement overtime request

Prepare time sheets

No

HR

Approval — No

Yes

Time sheets accepted

No

Yes

Calculate overtime hours & entitlements

Process overtime payment with monthly salary

Finance

* Indicates:
1- Reason of overtime 2- Required staff
3- Expected period

End

Appraising Performance

In Brief

1. People want and need feedback regarding how they are doing and appraisal provides an opportunity for you to give them that feedback.
2. before the appraisal, make sure to clarify the performance you expect so that the employee knows what he or she should be shooting for. Ask "What do I really expect this person to do?" 3- Performance appraisal tools include the graphic rating scale, alternation method, forced distribution method, BARS, MBO, and critical incident method.
4- Appraisal problems to beware of include unclear standards, halo effect, central tendency, leniency or strictness problem, and bias. .
5- Most subordinates probably want a specific explanation or examples regarding why they were appraised high or low, and for this, compiling a record of positive and negative critical incidents can be useful. Even if your firm requires that you summarize the appraisal in a form like a graphic rating scale, a list of critical incidents can be useful when the time comes to discuss the appraisal with your subordinate.
6. The subordinate should view the appraisal as a fair one, and in this regard there are four things to do: Evaluate his or her performance frequently; make sure you are familiar with the person's performance; make sure there is an agreement between you and your subordinate concerning his or her job duties; and finally, so- licit the person's help when you formulate plans for eliminating performance weaknesses.

7. There are three types of appraisal interviews. When performance is unsatisfactory but correctable the objective is to layout an action plan for correcting performance. For employees whose performance is satisfactory but for whom promotion is not possible the objective is to maintain satisfactory performance. Finally, the satisfactory-promotable interview has the main objective to discuss the person's career plans and to develop a specific action plan for the educational and professional development the person needs to move on to the next job.

8. to prepare for the appraisal interview, assemble the data, prepare the employee, and choose the time and place.

9. to bring about constructive change in your subordinate's behavior, get the person to talk in the interview. Try silence, use open-ended questions, state questions in terms of a problem, use a command question, use choice questions to try to understand the feelings underlying what the person is saying, and restate the person's last point as a question. On the other hand, don't do all the talking, don't use restrictive questions, don't be judgmental, don't give free advice, and don't get involved with name calling, ridicule, or sarcasm.

10. The best way to handle a defensive subordinate is to proceed very carefully. Specifically, recognize that defensive behavior is normal, never attack a person's defenses, postpone actions, and recognize your own limitations.

11. the most important thing you should aim to accomplish is to clear up job-related problems and set improvement goals and a schedule for achieving them.

12. Appraisals should also ideally serve a managing performance role by providing a concrete basis for an analysis of an employee's work-related performance. Creating more effective appraisals as described in this chapter is one way to accomplish this. Others suggest also taking a TQM-based approach. Characteristics of such an approach include: making the appraisal scale as broadly descriptive as possible so that it contains relatively few performance categories and avoids a forced distribution; measures results objectively; specifically identifies if the performance deficiency is a result of motivation, training, or factors outside the employee's control; uses 360 degree feedback; includes adequate samples of work behavior; addresses problems in an atmosphere of partnership and constructive advice; and bases performance standards on an analysis of key external and internal customers' needs and expectations.

POLICY OF PERFORMANCE APPRAISAL

There will be a performance appraisal after the three-month probation period by department's manager (as mentioned above

in the section of the probation period.)

There will be also a yearly performance appraisal for every employee by the department's manager. The appraisal will then be discussed with the employee to improve or adjust performance. In addition, salary adjustments, promotion and training recommendations will be made based on the appraisal.

Performance Appraisal Process

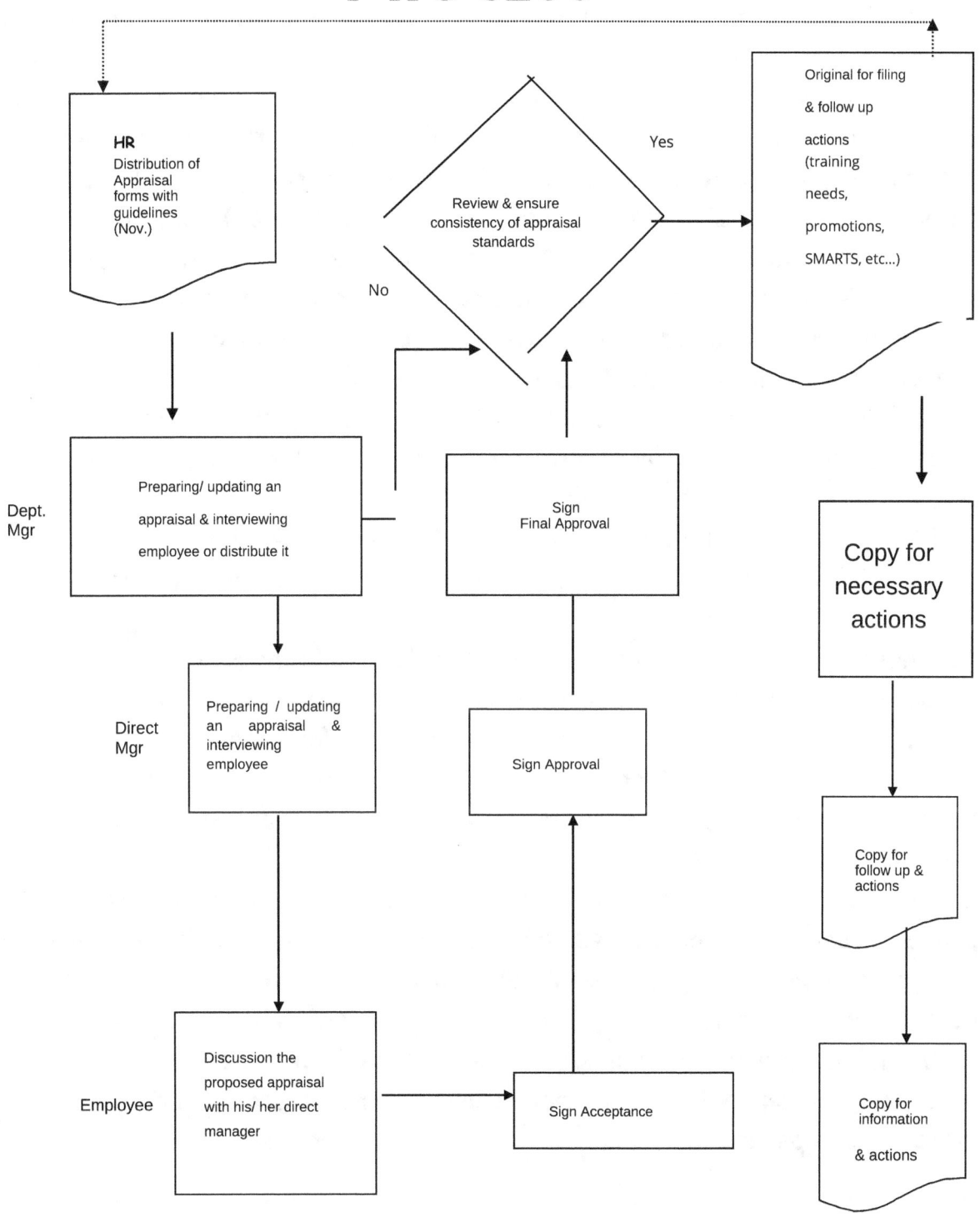

MANAGING CAREERS

In Brief

I. The key to managing your career is gaining insight into what you want out of a career, into your talents and limitations, and into your values and how they fit with the alternatives you are considering

2. The main stages in a person's career are: growth (roughly birth to age 14), exploration (roughly 15 to 24), establishment (roughly ages 24 to 44, the heart of most people's work lives), maintenance (45 to 65), and decline (pre-retirement).the establishment stage may consist of trial, stabilization, and mid-career crisis sub-stages. 3. the first step in planning your career is to learn as much as you can about your own interest, aptitudes, and skills. Start by identifying your occupational orientation: realistic, investigative, social, conventional, enterprising, and artistic. Then identify your skills and rank them from high to low.

4. Next identify your career anchors: technical/functional, managerial, creativity, autonomy, and security. Then ask yourself what you want to do.

5. There are many sources you can turn to for learning about occupations and careers. These include the Dictionary of Occupational Titles, the Occupational Outlook Handbook, Occupational Outlook Quarterly, the Encyclopedia of Careers and Vocational Guidance, and the Office of Personel Management's Handbook XI18.

6. The supervisor plays an important role in the career management process. Important guidelines include: Avoid reality shock, be demanding, and provide realistic job pre. Views, conduct career- oriented performance appraisals, and encourage job rotation

7. in making promotion decisions, you have to decide between seniority and competence, a formal or informal system, and ways to measure competence.

8. More firms today engage in practices aimed at helping employees "be all they can be," in other words, self-actualize. Training, job enrichment, and educational opportunities are examples. However, for many employees self-actualizing boils down to promotions and career progress. Many firms thus institute comprehensive career management/promotion-from-within programs.

9. Value-based hiring and developmental activities are two important components of such programs. Value-based hiring is important because promotion from within assumes you have employees who are promotable in the first place. Career developmental activities (including career assessment and planning) help employees identify their career interests and more intelligently plan career moves.

10. Career-oriented appraisals playa crucial role in managing careers. Here the super. Visor and employee link the latter's past performance, career ~references, and developmental needs to develop an appropriate career plan.

11. Career records/job posting systems are also important. Maintaining career-related data on employees and then openly posting all jobs ensure that the career goals and skills of inside candidates are matched openly and fairly with promotional opportunities.

Training & Career Development

The organization believes that the training of employees is necessary to operate successfully and to achieve overall organization's objectives, with full opportunities of updating and attaining skills at all levels. The department's manager and the Human Resources department determine the training needs. HR department selects the appropriate training methods and internal / external courses

The Basic Training process.

Any training program ideally consists of four steps, which are summarized in the following figure below. The purpose of the assessment step is to determine training needs which are basically determined in the performance appraisal form. Then, if one or more needs that can be covered through training are identified, training objectives should be set; here you specify in observable, measurable terms the performance you expect to obtain from employees who are trained. In the training step the actual training techniques are chosen and the training takes place. Finally, there should be an evaluation step. Here the trainees' pre- and post-training performances are compared, and the effectiveness of the training program is thus evaluated.

The Four Basic Steps in Training

```
┌─────────────────────────────────────┐
│            ASSESSMENT               │
│     What are the training needs     │
│     for this person and/or job?     │
└─────────────────────────────────────┘
                  │
                  ▼
┌─────────────────────────────────────┐
│      SET TRAINING OBJECTIVES        │
│        Objectives should be         │
│          observable and             │
│            measurable.              │
└─────────────────────────────────────┘
                  │
                  ▼
┌─────────────────────────────────────┐
│             TRAINING                │
│    Techniques include on-the-job    │
│    training, programmed learning.   │
└─────────────────────────────────────┘
                  │
                  ▼
┌─────────────────────────────────────┐
│    EVA LUATION Measure reaction,    │
│    learning, behavior, or results   │
└─────────────────────────────────────┘
```

TRAINING PROCESS

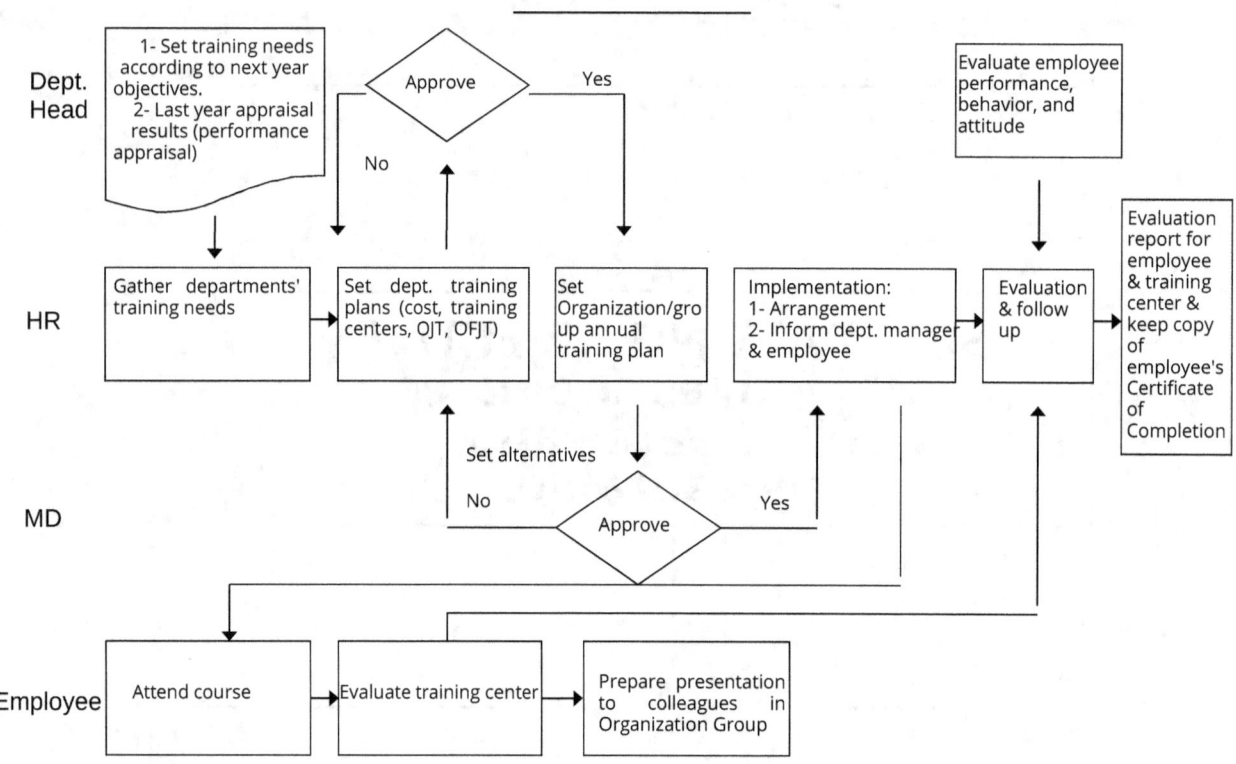

Dept. Head

1- Set training needs according to next year objectives.
2- Last year appraisal results (performance appraisal)

Approve — Yes / No

Evaluate employee performance, behavior, and attitude

HR

Gather departments' training needs

Set dept. training plans (cost, training centers, OJT, OFJT)

Set Organization/group annual training plan

Implementation:
1- Arrangement
2- Inform dept. manager & employee

Evaluation & follow up

Evaluation report for employee & training center & keep copy of employee's Certificate of Completion

MD

Set alternatives

No — Approve — Yes

Employee

Attend course

Evaluate training center

Prepare presentation to colleagues in Organization Group

Training procedures

1. Each department head sets the training needs for department staff according to department's objectives
and performance appraisal results using Training Needs Assessment Form.
2. HR department receives the training plans of all courses from different institutes/centers.
3. A training plan for all departments all over the year is set by HR department according to (availability of
subject, its topic, quality, cost, duration, timing, place, etc........)
4. Department's training plan is then discussed with concerned manager to be in line with department objectives
and Organization strategy and to assure that programs' content is suitable for employees' training needs.
5. Department manager will approve/not approve the whole annual plan for his department.

Training plan implementation:

1. After manager's approval on the plan and programs' content, the employee is informed with the topics of the
program.
2. HR sends a reservation of the training course to the center then sends the confirmation to the concerned
person & the department head.
3. HR receives the program invoice from the institute and sends it to finance for payment.
4. After completing training course, employee fills the Course Evaluation Form and sends it back to HR
department.
5. Employee delivers a copy of the trainee's certificate to HR for filing.
6. Department head fills the Follow up & Evaluation Form and send it to HR Department.
7. Employee prepares a course presentation to his colleagues.

Career Development & Promotions:

1.Promotions will be considered only in such instances where:
a) An employee is being charged with a broader mission/ increased scope of activity or any other
circumstances of greater responsibility with adequate knowledge, skill and ability.
b) ~~Availability of opportunity~~, such as new business, job transfer, promotion, resignations…etc. In this case
the organizational chart must be updated to indicate new promotions.
c) Such promotions will add value to the department & to career development process of the employee.
d) The employee may be eligible to the next promotion after at least three years of his last one (in
condition that s/he meets the above- mentioned conditions) unless in exceptional circumstances where it
may be sooner
2. Conversely, if an employee performs well in the grade he is in, there is no cause for promotion. In fact,
such satisfactory performance is the very confirmation that the employee in question is indeed in the proper
grade.
3. In case of an employee performing exceptionally well in his given responsibilities and within the grade s/he is
in, the organization bonus system will provide opportunity for adequate reward. There is no "automatic
increase" in grade due to the employee having performed satisfactorily in his/her grade over period of time.
4. In the course of ongoing appraisal discussions with the employee during mid-year appraisal (Section of
"supervisor's comments on self development of the employee" on page 6. of appraisal form), mention may be
made to the employee provided that conditions as outlined above under no. (1) Are existing, a promotion may
be considered.
5. The concerned manager should submit the following documents to HR Director:

o Updated organizational chart (after promotion)

o New job description (for the new position).

o Promotion form

6. In case of a change in individual responsibilities as outlined under no. (1) Above having been gradually and

successfully- introduced in preceding months, availability of opportunity and organization management

approval, and such promotion will be considered as per the 1st of January of any given year.

7. To avoid possible disappointment of the employee as well as eventual embarrassment to organization

management, no promises in this respect will be given to the employee in advance, instead a corresponding

remark may be made in the mid- year appraisal form.

8. Salary increase due to promotion will be according to organization salary grades structure.

Policy of Leaving the Organization

a. Termination:

In case of termination, attention should be paid to legal & financial issues.

b. Resignation:

• If the employee leaves the organization, s/he has to sign resignation letter 2 months before its due
date.

• HR conducts an exit interview with the resigned employee.

• In case employee persists on leaving the organization, clearance process starts as explained in
Resignation Process.

LEAVE POLICY: TERMINATION PROCESS

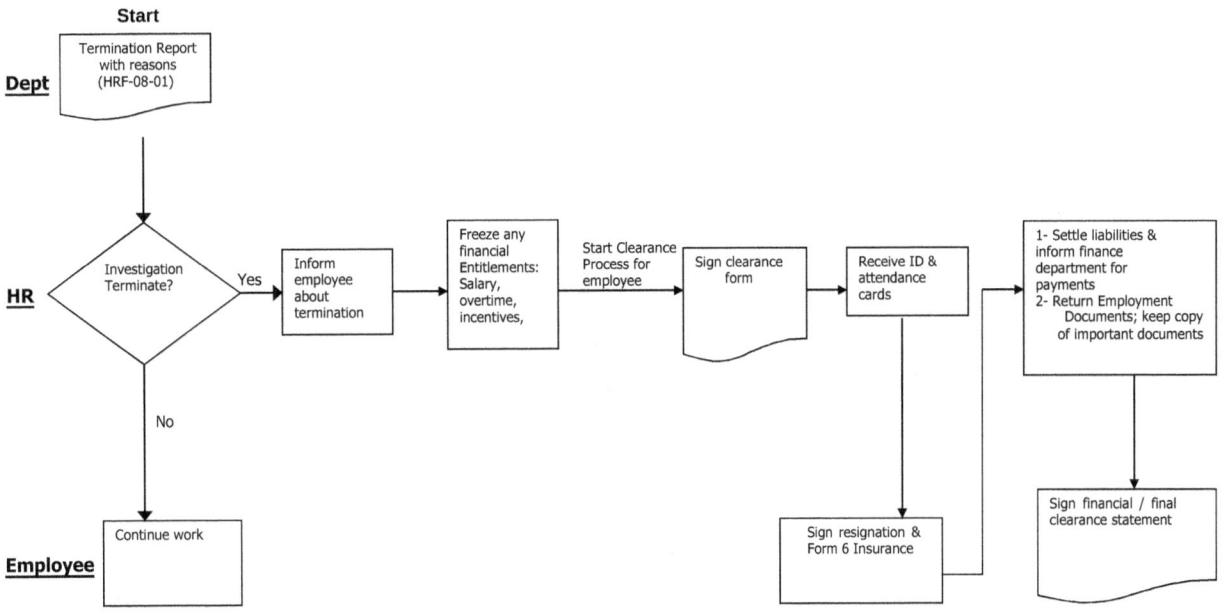

Dept

Start

Termination Report with reasons (HRF-08-01)

HR

Investigation Terminate?

Yes

Inform employee about termination

Freeze any financial Entitlements: Salary, overtime, incentives,

Start Clearance Process for employee

Sign clearance form

Receive ID & attendance cards

1- Settle liabilities & inform finance department for payments
2- Return Employment Documents; keep copy of important documents

No

Employee

Continue work

Sign resignation & Form 6 Insurance

Sign financial / final clearance statement

End

Leave Policy: Resignation Process

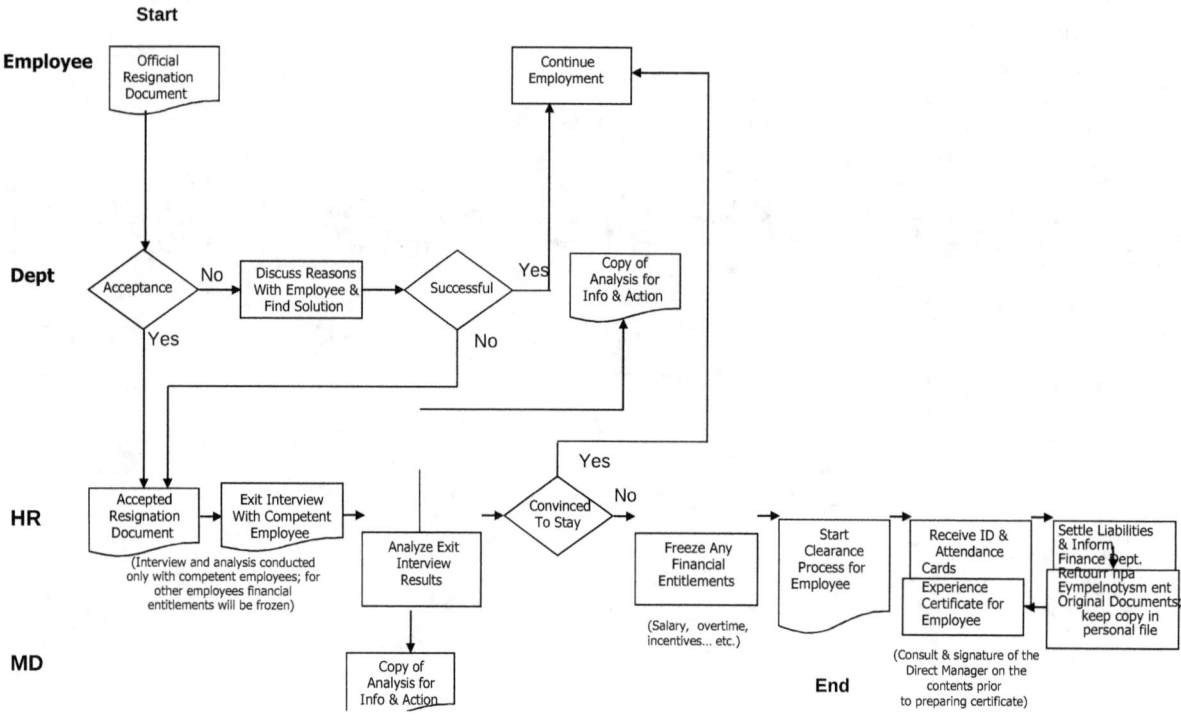

BENEFITS AND SERVICES

In Brief

1. The financial incentives we discussed are usually paid to specific employees whose work is above standard. Employee benefits, on the other hand, are available to all employees based on their membership in the organization. We discussed four types of benefit plans: pay supplements, insurance, retirement benefits, and services.

2. Supplemental pay benefits provide pay for time not worked. They include unemployment insurance, vacation and holiday pay, severance pay, and supplemental unemployment benefits.

3. Insurance benefits are another type of employee benefit. Worker's compensation, for example, is aimed at ensuring prompt income and medical benefits to work accident victims or their dependents regardless of fault. Most employers also provide! Group life insurance and group hospitalization, accident, and disability insurance.

4. Two types of retirement benefits were discussed: Social Security and pensions. Social Security does not just cover retirement benefits but survivors and disability! Benefits as well. There are three basic types of pension plans: group, deferred profit!

Sharing, and savings plans. One of the critical issues in pension planning is vesting the money that employer and employee have placed in the latter's pension fund, which cannot be forfeited for any reason. ERISA basically ensures that pension rights become vested and protected after a reasonable amount of time.

5. Most employers also provide benefits in the form of employee services. These include food services, recreational opportunities, legal advice, credit unions, and counseling.

6. Surveys suggest two conclusions regarding employees' preferences for benefits. First, time off (such as two extra weeks' vacation) seems to be the most preferred benefit. Second, the employee's age, marital status, and sex clearly influence his or her choice of benefits. (For example, younger employees were significantly more in favor of the family dental plan than were older employees.) This suggests the need for individualizing the organization's benefit plans.

7. the cafeteria approach allows the employee to put together his or her own benefit plan, subject to total cost limits and the inclusion of certain non-optional items. Several firms have installed cafeteria plans; they require considerable planning and computer assistance.

BENEFITS

1- Mobile Policy:

1-1 Mobile Telephone Lines:

Mobile telephone lines required by staff for business purposes are procured through HR department after prior authorization by Department Manager & MD.

1-2 Mobile monthly allowance:

Eligibility:

a- Managing Directors and Directors

b- Sales Managers

c- Sales Reps

d- Administration staff

Coverage	Local Calls	International Calls	Monthly Allowance LE	Payment Procedures
Senior Management (MD/Directors)	All covered	Business calls only	to HR Director - concerned cashier	· send mobile bills · HR Director and CFO review the bills and send them to the
Sales Managers	-	-		
Sales Reps	-	-		Paid with monthly salary
Administration Staff*	-	-		

Notes:

a- Organization does not provide mobile sets, lines, or cover any repairs costs.

b- Organization is not responsible for any problem that may result from using mobile phones while driving (accidents, license withdrawal…). Managers/Directors, therefore, must adhere to Egyptian Law which states that using mobile phones while driving is banned.

* Administration staff is eligible to mobile policy according to the following conditions:

o Business needs as recommended by direct supervisor.

o Approval of HR Director & MD.

2- Transportation:

Eligibility:

a- Managing Directors and Directors

b- Sales Managers

c- Sales Reps (a separate policy attached)

d- Administration staff

Coverage	Monthly Payment Procedures Allowance LE	
Senior (MD/Directors)	Management	Paid with monthly
Sales Managers	salary Car ownership	
Sales Reps	scheme	
Administration Staff	Actual Expenses using public transportation	

Policy & procedures for Managing Directors, Directors & Sales Managers:

a. The Organization provides eligible staff with a monthly transportation allowance against using their private
cars/public transportation in business affairs inside Egypt.

b. Allowance amount covers: fuel, car repair/maintenance, fines and renewal of car license.

c. Holidays during the month are deducted from allowance amount.

3- Medical Insurance (Proposal):

1. All employees are eligible to Medical Benefits.
2. there is a yearly coverage ceiling for each category of employees in which all medical services expenses are included:
   a. Category A: 30000 LE
   b. Category B: 22000 LE
   c. Category C: 15000 LE
3. Medical service provided to employees are as follows:

Category	Inside Hospital Treatment	Ambulance	External Clinics	Medicine
A	First Class/Single Room	100% of the cost	100% of the cost	100% of the cost
B	First Class/Single Room	100% of the cost	100% of the cost	100% of the cost
C	First Class/Double Room	100% of the cost	100% of the cost	100% of the cost

Category	Dental (LE/Year)	Eye Glasses (20% of participants & every 2 years) (LE/Year)	Monthly Treatment for chronic diseases	Critical Cases	Outside Medical Institution
A	900	400			In case of emergenc
B	600	350	10% of participants	y or places 2% of where participants medical services are not	
C	400	300			available

Other Items:

1. Pre-employment examination for all employees.
2. On-site weekly doctor visits.

4- Life Insurance (Proposal):

a- Normal Death:

Where an employee suffers death during service, the Organization provides a lump sum equal to the greater of the monthly final salary as at the date of death multiplied by the number of years of service of the employee. (Minimum payment 12 months)

_____

b- Complete Disability:

Where an employee suffers complete disability during service, the Organization provides a lump sum equal to the greater of the monthly final salary as at the date of death multiplied by the number of years of service of the employee. (Minimum payment 18 months)

c- Death Due to Accident:

For death by accident the Organization provides a lump sum equal to the greater of the monthly final salary as at the date of death multiplied by the number of years of service of the employee. (Minimum payment 24 months)

d- Retirement:

On retirement from employment the Organization shall provide employee with a lump sum equal to the final salary multiplied by the number of yeas of service in the Organization provided s/he spends 10 continuous years in Organization service

OTHER INFORMATION

1- Lost & Found/ Personal Property:

Any items of personal property that are lost or found in workplace should be reported at the HR/ security office.

2- Disciplinary Procedures:

The organization's policy and procedure on disciplinary matters and job performance is designed to protect the interests of the employees and the organization. The disciplinary procedure is based on the Labor Law no. 12 of 2003 and the Egyptian work and disciplinary regulations. Disciplinary action may be necessary where expected standards of job performance or behavior are not met, and aims to assist the employee to achieve and maintain the required standards of performance.

Minor faults will be dealt with informally, but when informal action has failed to produce the required improvement or when the matter is more serious, the department's head will use the following formal procedures. You may consult the Human Resources Department, which will normally be represented at these stages.

The procedure:

Stage One – Verbal Warning

Stage Two – Written Warning

Stage Three – Final Written Warning

Stage Four – Dismissal

If the employee feels that he/she has been unjustly disciplined, he/she may contact the Human Resources department.

Gross Misconduct:

The following are normally regarded as gross misconduct and which, if proven, may result in dismissal without notice. Gross misconduct includes: (but is not limited to):

1. Deliberate falsification of records.

2. Theft from the organization or any person on organization's workplace.

3. Any violation of account dealing rules including the giving or accepting of gifts or favors to or from suppliers, customers or officials.

4. Any serious breach of organization's rules or procedures.

5. Breach of confidentiality.

6. Serious carelessness that causes unacceptable loss, damage, or injury.

7. Serious acts of insubordination.

8. Fighting or attack on another person.

9. Deliberate damage to organization property.

10. Being convicted of a criminal offence which in the opinion of the organization proves unsuitability for further employment with the organization.

11. Serious incapability through alcohol or being under the influence of illegal drugs or other prescribed substances at any time during the working day (whether or not in workplace)

12. Behaving harmfully to the good name of the organization and/or any group organization.

13. Any misrepresentation or false statement made during the job application process relating to a person's own work or that of a colleague.

14. Racial or disability discrimination (including harassment) of another employee, agency or any client of the organization, visitor to the organization's premises or any other party to whom the organization may have a duty to prevent such discrimination.

Serious Misconduct:

The following are normally regarded as serious misconduct and which, if proven, may result in final written warning. For further or repeated offence, subsequent stages in disciplinary procedure will be used. Serious misconduct includes (but not limited to):

1. Refusal to carry out reasonable requests or instructions.

2. Repeated absences from work without permission.

General Misconduct:

The following are normally regarded as general misconduct and which, if proven, may result in written warning. For further or

repeated offence, stages in disciplinary procedure will be used. General misconduct includes (but not limited to):
1. Unsatisfactory record of attendance or reliability.
2. Repeated lateness.
3. Failure to maintain acceptable standards of dress.
4. Poor work performance.
5. Poor standard of personal hygiene.

3- Employees' Complaints Procedures:

If at any time during employment with the organization, an employee has a problem or complaint, every attempt should be made to resolve it informally. In circumstances where this is not possible, the employee can follow a formal procedure, which is conducted in complete confidence.

The procedure:

Stage One:

The employee should explain out his/her complaint in writing and give it to department's manager/supervisor who will arrange a meeting to consider the matter. It is hopped that the matter will be resolved at this meeting.

Stage Two:

If the matter is not resolved at stage one, the complaint should be passed on in writing to the next level of management. The complaint will be discussed both with the employee and the manager/supervisor within ten working days of the meeting at stage one, unless there is a good reason for delay.

Stage Three:

In those cases where the matter remains unresolved, the employee may appeal to the top management where decision made will be final.

General points:

o To avoid any possibility of misunderstanding and misinterpretation, the complaint must be reported in writing.

o At each stage of the complaint procedures the employee concerned may be accompanied by a colleague of his/her choice if he/she requires.

o Human Resources department is able to give advice to employees about complaint procedures, and may be contacted for discussion at any stage during the process.

4- Confidentiality of Information during and after Employment:

What an employee see or hear in the organization, stays in the organization. During an employee's employment and if his employment has ended, s/he shall not directly or indirectly use or disclose to third parties, other than in the proper performance of his/her duties for the organization, any of the secrets and confidential information of the organization or any other group organization. Upon hiring, all employees are obliged to keep work date and information confidential as mentioned in article no. 15 in Employment Contract.

5- Other Employment (working with others):

As an organization employee, employees are not permitted either to accept or continue any employment other than for the organization. In exceptional circumstances, applications made by employees to take up or continue other employment may be considered provided that there is an added value to the organization, the department's manager is satisfied that such employment does not interfere or conflict with responsibilities to the organization and on the understanding that the organization may withdraw its approval at any time. Any agreement to take up or continue outside employment or appointment must be registered with the Human Resources Department.

6- Notice Periods:

In case of employment termination for any reason, the employee will be given, in writing, the following period of notice:
o During probation period: no notice period
o Thereafter and before completion of 12 months: two month
In case any employee leaves the organization, two months period of notice has to be given.

7- Return of Organization Property:

Upon end of employment for any reason, employee will immediately deliver to the organization all the property- including but not limited to documents, software, and keys belonging to the organization or in his/her possession or under his/her control.

GLOSSARY

Management Process:
The five basic functions of planning, organizing, staffing, leading, controlling.

Human Resources Management
The policies & practices one needs to carry out the "people" or Human resources aspects of a management position , including recruiting, screening, training, rewarding, and appraisal.

Authority
The rights to make decisions, direct others' work, and give orders.

Line manager
A manager who is authorized to direct the work of subordinates and responsible for accomplishing the organization's goals.

Staff Manager
A manager who assists and advises line manager.

Implied Authority;
The authority exerted by a personnel manager by virtue of others' knowledge that s/he has access to top management (in areas like testing and affirmative action)

Functional control
The authority exerted by an HR manager as coordinator of personnel activities.

The function of an HR manager in assisting and advising line management.

Globalization

The tendency of firms to extend their sales or manufacturing to new markets abroad.

2-Equal opportunity & the law

Title VII of the 1964 Civil Rights Act

The section of the act that says an employer cannot discriminate on the basis of race, color, religion, sex, or national origin with respect to employment.

Equal Employment opportunity commission (EEOC)

The commission created by Title VII, is empowered to investigate job discrimination complaints and sue on behalf of complaints.

Affirmative action

Steps that are taken for the purpose of eliminating the present effects of past discrimination.

Office of Federal contract compliance programs (OFCCP)

This office is responsible for implementing the executive orders and ensuring compliance of Federal Contractors.

Equal Pay Act of 1963

The act requiring equal pay for equal work, regardless of sex.

Vocational Rehabilitation Act of 1973

The act requiring certain federal contractors to take affirmative action for disabled persons.

School Board of Nassau County v. Airline.

U.S. Supreme court ruling that persons with contagious diseases are covered by the Vocational Rehabilitation Act of 1973.

Vietnam Era Veterans' Readjustment Act of 1974

An Act requiring that employers with government contracts take affirmative action to hire disabled veterans.

Pregnancy Discrimination Act (PDA)

An amendment to Title VII of the Civil Rights act that prohibits sex discrimination based on "pregnancy childbirth, or related medical conditions".

Federal Agency guidelines

Guidelines issued by federal agencies charged with ensuring compliance with equal employment federal legislation explaining recommended employer procedures in detail.

Sexual harassment

Harassment on the basis of sex that has the purpose or effect of substantially interfering with a person's work performance or creating an intimidating, hostile, or offensive work environment.

Merit or Savings Bank, FSBv. Vinson

U.S. Supreme Court's first decision on sexual harassment holding that existence of a hostile environment even without economic hardship is sufficient to prove harassment even if participation was voluntary.

The procedure for determining the duties the duties and skill requirements of a job and the kind of person who should be hired for it.

Job description

A list of job's duties, responsibilities, reporting relationships, working conditions, and supervisory responsibilities- one product of job analysis.

Diary/logs

Daily listings made by workers of every activity in which they engage along with the time each activity takes.

Position analysis questionnaire (PAQ)

A questionnaire used to collect quantifiable data concerning the duties and responsibilities of various jobs.

Department of labor job analysis

Standardized method for rating, classifying, and comparing virtually every kind of job based on data, people, and things.

Functional job analysis.

A method for classifying jobs similar to the department of labor job analysis but additionally taking into account the extent to which instructions reasoning, judgment, and verbal facility are necessary for performing job tasks.

Study of a firm's past employment needs over a period of years to predict future needs.

Ratio analysis

A forecasting technique for determining future staff needs by using ratios between sales volume and number of employees needed.

Scatter plot

A graphical method used to help identify the relationship between two variables.

Computerized forecast

The determination of future staff needs by projecting a firm's sales, volume of production and personnel required to maintain this volume of output using computers and software packages.

Qualifications inventories

Manual or computerized systematic records listing employees' education, career, and development interests ,languages, special skills, and so on to be used in forecasting inside candidates for promotion.

Personnel replacement charts

Company records showing present performance and promotion ability of inside candidates for the most important positions.

Position replacement card

A card prepared for each position in a company to show possible replacement candidates & their qualifications.

Job posting

Posting notices of job openings on company bulletin boards is an effective recruiting method.

The accuracy with which a test, interview, and so on, measures what it is purports to measure or fulfills the function it was designed to fill.

Criterion validity

A type of validity based on showing that scores on the test (predictors) are related to job performance (criterion)

Content validity

A test that is content valid is one in which the test contains fair sample of the tasks and skills actually needed for the job in question.

Reliability

The characteristics which refers to the consistency of scores obtained by the same person when retested with the identical or equivalent tests.

Expectancy chart

A graph showing the relationship between test scores & job performance for a large group of people.

Work samples

Actual job tasks used in testing applicants' performance.

Work sampling technique

A testing method based on measuring performance on actual basic job tasks.

Management assessment centers

A situation in which management candidates are asked to make decisions in hypothetical situations and are scored on their performance. It is also involves testing and the use of management games.

An unstructured conversational- style interview. The interviewer pursues points of interests as they come up in response to questions.

Directive interview

An interview following a set sequence of questions.

Stress interview

An interview in which the applicant is made uncomfortable by a series of often rude questions. This technique helps identify hypersensitive applicants and those with low or high stress tolerance.

Appraisal interview:

A discussion following a performance appraisal in which supervisor and employee discuss the employee's rating and possible remedial actions.

Situational interview

A series of job-related questions which focuses on relevant past job-related behaviors.

Serialized interview

An interview in which the applicant is interviewed sequentially by several persons and each rates the applicant on a standard form.

Panel interview

An interview in which a group of interviewers question the applicant.

7- Orienting and training Employee orientation

A procedure for providing new employee with basic background information about the firm.

Reality shock

That state which results from the discrepancy between what the new employees expected from his/her new job, and the realities of it.

Training

The process of teaching new employees the basics skills they need to perform their jobs.

Task analysis

A detailed study of a job to identify the skills required so that an appropriate training program may be instituted.

Performance analysis

Verifying that there is a performance deficiency and determining whether that deficiency should be rectified through training or through some other means (such as transferring the employee)

On-the-job training (OJT)

Training a person to learn a job while working at it.

Job instruction training (JIT)

Listing of each job's basic tasks, along with key points in order to provide step-by-step training for employees.

Programmed learning

A systematic method for teaching job skills involving presenting questions or facts, allowing the person to respond, and giving the learner immediate feedback on the accuracy of his/ her answers.

Vestibule or simulated training

Training employees on special off-the-job equipment, as in airplane pilot training, whereby training costs & hazards can be reduced.

Worker involvement programs

Programs that aim to boost organizational effectiveness by getting employees to participate in planning, organizing, and managing their jobs.

Controlled experimentation

Formal method of testing the effectiveness of a training program, preferably with before-and-after tests and a control group.

Any attempt to improve current or future management performance by imparting knowledge, changing attitudes, or increasing skills.

Succession planning

A process through which senior-level openings are planned for & eventually filled.

Job rotation

A management training technique that involves moving a trainee from department to department to broaden his/her experience and identify strong & weak points.

Junior board

A method of providing middle – management trainees with experience inn analyzing company problems by inviting them to set on a junior board of directors &and make recommendations on overall company policies.

Action learning

A training technique by which management trainees are allowed to work fulltime analyzing and solving problems in other departments.

Case study method

A development method in which the manager is presented with a written description of an organizational problem to diagnose and solve.

Management game

A development technique in which teams of managers compete with one anther by making computerized decision regarding realistic but simulated companies.

Role playing

A training technique in which trainees act out the parts of people in realistic management situation.

Behavior modeling

A training technique in which trainees are first shown good management techniques in film, are then asked to play roles in a simulated situation, and then given feedback and praise by their supervisor.

In-house development centers

A company-based method exposing prospective managers to realistic exercises to develop improved management skills.

Organizational development (OD)

A method aimed at changing the attitudes, values, and beliefs, of employees so that employees can improve the organization.

Survey feedback

A method that involves surveying employees' attitude and providing feedback to department managers so that problems can be solved by the managers and employees.

Sensitivity training

A method for increasing employees' insights into their own behavior by candid discussions in groups led by special trainers.

Team building

Improving the effectiveness of teams such as corporate officers and divisions directors through use of consultants, interviews, and team-building meetings.

Managerial grid

A matrix that represents different possible leadership styles.

A plan whereby employees build their workday around a core of midday hours.

Four-day workweek

An arrangement that allows employees to work four ten-hour days instead of the more usual five eight- hour days.

Job sharing

A concept that allows two or more people to share a single full-time job.

Telecommuting

A work arrangement in which employees work at remote locations, usually at home, using video displays, computers, and other telecommunications equipment to carry out their responsibilities.

Flex years

A work arrangement under which employees can choose (at six-month intervals) the number of hours they want to work each month over the next year.

Quality circle

A group of five to ten specially trained employees who meet on a regular basis to identify and solve problems in their work area.

Self-directed teams

Highly trained work groups that use consensus decision making & broad authority to self-direct their activities.

10- Appraising performance. Graphic rating scale

A scale that lists a number of traits and a range of performance for each. The employee is then rated by identifying the score that best describes his/her level of performance for each trait.

Alternation ranking method

Ranking employees from best to worst on a particular trait.

Paired comparison method

Ranking employees by making a chart of all possible pairs of employees for each trait and indicating which the better employee of the pair is.

Forced distribution method.

Similar to grading on a curve; predetermined percentages of rates are placed in various performance categories.

Critical incident method.

Keeping a record of uncommonly good or undesirable examples of an employee's work-related behavior and reviewing it with the employee at predetermined times.

Behaviorally anchored rating scale (BARS)

An appraisal method that aims at combining the benefits of narrative critical incidents and quantified ratings by anchoring a quantified scale with specific narrative examples of good poor and performance.

Management by objectives. (MBO)

nvolves setting specific measurable goals with each employee and then periodically reviewing progress made.

Unclear performance standards.

An appraisal scale that is too open to interpretation; instead include descriptive phrases that define each trait and what is meant by standards like "good" or "unsatisfactory".

Halo effect

In performance appraisal the problem that occurs when a supervisor"s rating of a subordinate on one trait biases the rating of that person on other traits.

Central tendency

A tendency to rate all employees the same way such as rating them all average.

Strictness/leniency

The problem that occurs when a supervisor has a tendency to rate all subordinates either high or low.

Bias

The tendency to allow individual differences such as race, age, and sex to affect the appraisal rates theses receive.

Appraisal interview

An interview in which the supervisor and subordinate review the appraisal and makes plans to remedy deficiencies and reinforce strengths.

Career planning & development the deliberate process through which a person becomes aware of personal career-related attributes and the lifelong series of stages that contribute to his/her career fulfillment.

Career cycle

The stages through which a person career evolves.

Growth stage

The period from birth to age 14 during the person develops a self-concept by identifying with and interacting with other people such as family, friends, and teachers.

Exploration stage.

The period from birth to ages 15-24 during which a person seriously explores various occupational alternatives, attempting to match these alternatives with her/her interests and abilities.

Establishment stage

The period, roughly from ages 24 to 44, that is the heart of most people's work life.

Trial sub stage

The period from about age 25 to 30 during which the person determining whether or not the chosen field is suitable and if it is not attempts to change it.

Stabilization sub stage

The period, roughly from age 30 to 40, during which firm occupational goals are set and more explicit career planning is made to determine the sequence for accomplishing these goals.

Midcareer crisis sub stage

The period occurring between mid-thirties and mid-forties during which often make major reassessment of their progress relative to their original career ambitions and goals.

Maintenance stage

The period from about ages 45 to 65 during which the person secures his/her place in the world of work.

Decline stage

The period during which many people are faced with the prospect of having to accept reduced levels of power and responsibility.

Occupational orientation

The theory developed by John Holland that says there are six basic personal orientations that determine the sorts of careers to which people are drawn.

Occupational skills

The skills needed to be successful in particular occupation. According to the Dictionary of Occupational Titles., occupational skills break down into three groups depending on whether they emphasize data, people, or things.

Aptitudes

Innate abilities which include intelligence, numerical aptitude, mechanical, comprehension, and manual dexterity, as well as talents such as artistic, theatrical, or musical ability that plays an important role in career decisions.

Career anchors

A concern or value that you will not give up if a choice has to be made.

Reality shocks.

Results of a period that may occur at the initial career entry when the new employee's high job expectations confront the reality of boring, unchallenging job.

All forms of pay or rewards going to employees and arising from their employment.

Davis-Bacon Act

A law passed in 1931 that sets wage rates for laborers employed by contractors working for the federal government.

Walesh- Healy Public Contract Act.

A law enacted in 1936 that requires minimum-wage and working conditions for employees working on any government contract amounting to more than$ 10.000.

Fair Labor Standard Act

Congress passed this act in 1936 to provide for minimum wages, maximum hours, overtime pay, and child labor protection. The law has been amended many times and covers most employees.

Equal Pay Act of 1963

An amendment to the Fair labor Standards Act designed to require equal pay for women doing the same work as men.

Civil Rights Act

This law makes it illegal to discriminate in employment because of race, color, religion, sex, or national origin.

Employee Retirement Income Security Act (ERISA)

The law that provides government protection of pensions for all employees with company pension plans. It also regulates vesting rights (employees who leave before retirement may claim compensation from the pension plan).

Salary survey

A survey aimed at determining prevailing wage rates. A good salary survey provides specific wage rate for specific jobs. Formal written questionnaire surveys are the most comprehensive, but telephone surveys and newspaper ads are also source of information.

Benchmark job

A job that Is used to anchor the employer's pay scale and around which other jobs are arranged in order of relative worth.

Job evaluation

A systematic comparison done in order to determine the worth of one job relative to anther.

Compensable factor

A fundamental, compensable element of a job, such as skills, effort, responsibility, and working conditions.

Ranking method

The simple method of job evaluation that involves ranking each job relative to all other jobs usually based on overall difficulty.

Classification (or grading) method

A method for categorizing jobs into groups.

Classes

Dividing jobs into classes based on set of rules for each class, such as amount of independent judgments, skill, physical effort, and so forth, required for each class of jobs. Classes usually contain similar jobs such all secretaries.

Grades

A job classification system synonymous with class, although grades often contain dissimilar jobs, such as secretaries, mechanics, and fight fighters. Grade descriptions are written based on compensable factors listed in classification systems, such as the federal classification system.

Grade Description

Written description of the level of say, responsibility and knowledge required by jobs in each grade. Similar jobs can then be combined into grades or classes.

Point method

The job evaluation method in which a number of compensable factors are identified and then the degree to which each of these factors is present in the job is determined

Factor comparison method

A widely used method of ranking jobs according to a variety of skill and difficulty factors, then adding up these ranking to arrive at an overall numerical rating for each given job.

Pay grade

A pay grade is comprised of jobs of approximately equal difficulty.

Wage curve

Shows the relationship between the value of the job and the average wage paid for this job.

Rate ranges

A series of steps or levels within a pay grade usually based upon years of service.

Comparable worth

The concept by which women who are usually paid less than men can claim that men in comparable rather than strictly equal jobs are paid more.

Fredrick Taylor's observation that haphazard setting of piece work requirement & wages by supervisors was not sufficient, and that careful study was needed to define acceptable production quota for each job.

Scientific management

The careful, scientific study of the job for the purpose of posting productivity and job satisfaction.

Spot bonus

A spontaneous incentive awarded to individuals for accomplishment not readily measured by standard.

Variable pay

Any plan that ties pay to productivity or profitability, usually as one-time lump payments.

Piecework

A system of pay based on the number of items processed by each individual worker in a unit of time, .such as items per hour or items per day .

Straight piecework plan

Under this pay system each worker receives a set payment for each piece produced or processed in a factory or shop.

Guaranteed piecework plan

The minimum hourly wage plus an incentive for each piece produced above a set number of pieces per hour.

Standard hour plan

A plan by which a worker is paid by basic hourly rate but is paid an extra percentage of his/her base rates for production exceeding the standard per hour or per day. Similar to piecework payment but based on a percent premium.

Team or group incentive plan

A plan in which a production standard is set for a specific work group, and its members are paid incentives if the group exceeds the production standard.

Annual bonus

Plans that are designed to motivate short-term performance of managers and are tied to company profitability.

Capital accumulation programs

Long-term incentives most often reserved for senior executives. Six popular plans include stock options, stock appreciations rights, performance achievement plans, phantom stock plans, and book value plans.

Stock options

The right to purchase a stated number of shares of company stock at today's price at some time in the future.

Merit pay (merit raise)

Any salary increase awarded to an employee based on his/her individual performance.

Profit-sharing plan

A plan whereby most employees share in the company's profits

Employee stock ownership plan (ESOP)

A corporation contributes shares of its own stock to trust in which additional contributions are made annually. The trust distributes the stock to employees on retirement or separation from service.

Scanlon plan

An incentive plan developed in 1937 by Joseph Scanlon and designed to encourage cooperation, involvement, and sharing of benefits.

Gain sharing plan

An incentive plan that engages employees in a common effort to achieve productivity objectives.

14- Benefits and services. Benefits

Indirect financial payments given to employees. They may include health and life insurance, vacation, pension, education, plans, and discounts on company products, for instance.

Supplemental pay benefits.

Benefits for time not worked such as unemployment insurance, vacation and holiday pay, and sick pay

Unemployment insurance.

Provides weekly benefits if a person is unable to work through some fault other than his/her own.

Sick leave

Provides pay to an employee when he/she is out of work because of illness.

Severance pay

A one-time payment some employers provide when terminating an employee.

Supplemental unemployment benefits

Provide for a "guaranteed annual income" in certain industries where employers must shut down to change machinery or reduced work. These benefits are paid by the company and supplement unemployment benefits.

Worker's compensation

Provides income and medical benefits to work-related accident victims on their dependents regardless of fault.

Group life insurance

Provides lower rates for the employer or employee and including all employees regardless of health or physical condition.

Health Maintenance organization (HMO)

A prepaid health care system that generally provides routine round-the-clock medical services as well as preventive medicine in a clinic-type arrangement for employees, who pay a nominal fee in addition to the fixed annual fee the employer, pays.

Preferred Provider Organizations (PPOs)

Groups of health care providers that contract with employers, insurance companies, or third party payers to provide medical care services at a reduced fee.

Pregnancy Discrimination Act (PDA)

An amendment to the Title VII of the Civil Right Act that prohibits sex discrimination based on " pregnancy, childbirth, or related medical conditions" it requires employers to provide benefits-including sick leave & disability benefits and health and medical insurance – the same as for any employee not able to work because of disability.

Social Security

Provides three types of benefits: retirement income at the age of 62 and thereafter; survivor's or death benefits payable to the employee's dependents regardless of age at time of death; and disability benefits payable to disabled employees and their dependents. These benefits are payable only if the employee insured under the Social E\Security Act.

Pension plans

Plans that provides a fixed sum when employees reach a predetermined retirement age or when they can no longer work due to disability.

Defined benefit pension plan.

A plan that contains formula for determining retirement benefits

Defined contribution plan

A plan in which the employer's contribution to employees' retirement or savings funds is specified.

Deferred profit-sharing plan

A plan in which a certain amount of profits is credited to each employee's account, payable at retirement, termination, or death.

Vesting

Provision that money placed in a pension fund cannot be forfeited for any reason.

Employee Retirement Income Security Act (ERISA)

Signed into law by President Ford in1974 to require that pension rights be vested, and protected by a government agency, PBGC. Pension Benefits Guarantee Corporation (PBGC)
Established under ERISA to ensure that pensions meet vesting obligations; also insures pension should a plan terminate without sufficient funds to meet its vested obligations.

Golden Offerings

Offers to current employees aimed at encouraging them to retire early, perhaps even with the same pension they would expect if they retired at; say, age65.

Early retirement window

A type of golden offering by which employees are encouraged to retire early, the incentive being liberal pension benefits plus perhaps a cash payment.

Employee Assistance Program (EAP)

A formal employer program for providing employees with counseling and/or treatment programs for problems such as alcoholism, gambling, or stress.

A form of union security in which the company can hire only union members. This was outlawed in 1947 but still exists in some industries (such as printing).

Union shop

A form of union security in which the company can hire nonunion people but they must join the union after a prescribed period of time and pay dues. (If they do not, they can be fired)

Agency shop

A form of union security in which employees that do not belong to the union must still pay union dues on the assumption that union efforts benefit all workers.

Open shop

Perhaps the least attractive type of union security from the union's point of view, the workers decide whether or not join the union; and those who join must pay dues.

Norris-LaGuardia Act

This law marked the beginning of the era of strong encouragement of unions and guaranteed to each employee the right to bargain collectively "free from interference, restraint, or coercion"

National labor Relations Board (NLRB)

The agency created by the Wagner Act to investigate unfair labor practice charges and to provide for secret-ballot elections and majority rule in determining whether or not a firm's employees want a union.

National Labor Relations (or Wagner Act)

This law banned certain types of unfair labor practices and provided for secret-ballot elections and majority rule for determining whether or not a firm's employees want to
Unionize.

Taft-Hartley Act

Also known as the labor Management Relations Act, this law prohibited union unfair labor practices and enumerated the rights of the employees as union members. It also enumerated the rights of employers.

National emergency strikes

Strikes that might "imperil the national health and safety."

Landrum-Griffin Act

The law aimed at protecting union members from possible wrongdoing on the part of their union.

Authorization cards

In order to petition for a union election, the union must show that at least 30% of employees may be interested in being unionized. Employees indicate this interest by signing authorization cards.

Bargaining unit

The group of employees the union will be authorized to represent.
Collective bargaining
The process through which representatives of management and the union meet to negotiate a labor agreement.

Good faith bargaining

A term that means both parties are communicating and negotiating and that proposal are being matched with both parties making every reasonable effort to arrive at agreements. It does not mean that either party is compelled to agree to a proposal.

Voluntary bargaining items

Items in collective bargaining over which bargaining is neither illegal nor mandatory –neither party can be compelled against its wishes to negotiate over those items.

Illegal bargaining items.

Items in collective bargaining that are forbidden by law; for example, the clause agreeing to hire " union members exclusively" would be illegal in a right-to-work-state.

Mandatory bargaining items

Items in collective bargaining that a party must bargain over if they are introduced by other party- for example, pay.

Mediation

Intervention in which a neutral third party tries to assist the principals in reaching agreement.

Arbitration

The most definitive type of third-party intervention, in which the arbitrator usually has the power to determine and dictate the settlement terms.

Wildcat strike

An unauthorized strike occurring during the term of a contract.

Sympathy strike

A strike that takes place when one union strikes in support of the strike of another.

Boycott

The combined refusal by employees and other interested parties to buy or use the employer's products.

Communications programs that allow employees to register questions, concern, and complaints about work-related matters.

Opinion surveys

Communication devices that use questionnaires to regularly ask employees their opinions about the company, management, and work life.

Top-down programs

Communications activities including in-house television centers, frequent roundtable discussions and in-house newsletters that provide continuing opportunities for the firm to let all employees be up-dated on important matters regarding the firm.

Guaranteed fair treatment.

Employer programs that are aimed at ensuring that all employees are treated fairly, generally by providing formalized, well documented, and highly publicized vehicles through which employees can appeal any eligible issues.

Open-door program

IBM's fair treatment program, which gives every IBM employee the right to appeal this actions of his/her supervisor by taking the concern successively higher level of management.

Discipline

A procedure that corrects or punishes a subordinate because a rule or procedure has been violated.

Dismissal

Involuntary termination of an employee's employment with the firm

Insubordination

Willful disregard or disobedience of the boss's authority or legitimate orders; criticizing the boss in public.

Termination at will

The idea, based in law that the employment relationship can be terminated at will by either the employer or the employee for any reason.

Wrongful discharge

An employee dismissal that does not comply with the law or does not comply with the contractual agreement stated or implied by the firm via its employment application forms, employee manuals, or other promises.

Termination interview

The interview in which an employee is informed of the fact that s/he has been dismissed.

Outplacement counseling

A systematic process by which a terminated person is trained and counseled in the techniques of self-appraisal and securing a new position.

Plant closing law

The worker Adjustment and Retraining Notification Act. Which requires notification employees in the event an employer decides to close its facility?

A situation in which there is a temporary shortage of work and employees are told that there is no work for them but that management intends to recall them when work is again available.

Bumping/layoff procedures

Detailed procedures that determine who will be laid off if no work is available; generally allow employees to use their seniority to remain on the job.

Voluntary reduction in pay plan

An alternative to layoffs in which all employees agree to reductions in pay to keep every one working.

Voluntary time off

An alternative to layoffs in which some employees agree to take time off to reduce the employer's pay roll and avoid the need for a layoff.

Rings of defense

An alternative layoff plan in which temporary supplemental employees are hired with the understanding that may be laid off at any time.

Downsizing

Refers to the process of reducing, usually dramatically the number of people employed by the firm.

Lifetime employment without guarantees

Refers to a commitment on the part of firms like Toyota and Saturn to do all that reasonably possible to avoid layoffs and non-performance- based dismissals while recognizing that ultimately the employment relationship must be at will.

Retirement

The point at which at which a person gives up one's work usually between the ages of 60 to 65 ,but increasingly earlier today due to firm 'early retirement incentive plans.

17-Employee safety and Health Occupational Safety and Health Act

The law passed by Congress in 1970 "to assure so far possible every working man and woman in the nation safe and healthful working conditions and to preserve our human resources"

Occupational Safety and Health Administration (OSHA)

The agency created within the department of Labor to set safety and health standards for almost all workers in the United States.

Citations

Summons informing employers and employees of the regulations and standards that have been violated in the workplace.

Unsafe conditions

The mechanical and physical conditions that cause accidents.

Unsafe acts

Behavior tendencies and undesirable attitudes that cause accidents.

Burnout

The total depletion of physical and mental resources caused by excessive striving to reach an unrealistic work-related goal.

www.ingramcontent.com/pod-product-compliance
Lightning Source LLC
Chambersburg PA
CBHW082220290526
45794CB00009B/3609